THE GRATITUDE REVOLUTION

How To Love Your Life and Be Inspired By The World Around You

By Laura Moreno

First Edition, 2017
Edited by Joshua A. Firger
ISBN 9781521170816

Laura Moreno
183 Adelphi St.
Brooklyn, NY 11205
United States
www.lauramoreno.com

Dedicated to my dear husband Josh and to my gorgeous family and friends all over the world!

*"If the only prayer you say in your life is
"Thank You" that would suffice."
Meister Eckhart (1260-1327)*

TABLE CONTENTS

BONUS

Enter your email to receive a pdf with 30 of my favorite Gratitude Quotes that will inspire you and make you happier while reading this book.

To receive a copy of your Gratitude Quotes pdf document, go to: https://s.privy.com/348jIWk

INTRODUCTION

"It is not happy people who are thankful. It is thankful people who are happy."
Author Unknown

In the next 10 years, millions of people will become happier using the power of Gratitude and after reading this book you will be one of them.

Every happy person has a secret that they are not telling you. This secret lets them change their mood instantly, enjoy better health, earn more money and be happier.

In the next pages we will reveal this secret, tell you why and how it works and give you some exercises to power your joy for living.

What immediate benefits will you see?

"Humanity is coming to recognize that it is impossible to be grateful and hateful at the same time." Nina Lesowitz, author of "Living Life as a Thank You"

These are some of the hundreds of benefits you will see:

- You will be happier instantly
- You're going to start smiling more
- You're going to start seeing the positive side of things more often
- You're going to be healthier
- You'll attract more positive and happy people

- You will be more successful at work
- You will have more energy

"You will laugh a lot and love a lot more. You will draw more and more positive people into your life. You will be healthier physically. You will be happy to be alive." Susan Jeffers, author of *"Feel the Fear and Do It Anyway"*

Who is this book for?

This book is for anyone who:

- Wants to be happier
- Wants to find the joy of living
- Wants to attract love to their life
- Wants to get over a loss
- Wants to feel like a child

What will you find in this book?

This book is divided into 3 sections

Part 1 - Introduction to Gratitude: In this first section we talk about the definition of Gratitude (Chapter 1) and some of its wonderful benefits (Chapter 2).
Part 2 - A Practical Guide to Gratitude: This middle section will give you all the tools you need to practice Gratitude (Chapter 3), setup your Gratitude routine (Chapter 4), and evaluate your life so you know better the areas that you need to work on (Chapter 5)
Part 3 - An Inspirational Guide to Gratitude: In this last section we focus on all the things you can be grateful for (Chapter 6)

In each of the chapters of this book you can find:

- A little bit of theory and studies about Gratitude
- Awesome quotes from some amazing people
- Stories of grateful people and how Gratitude shaped their lives
- A Gratitude exercise: doing these exercises will increase your

happiness immensely!
- A chapter summary

About me

"I can't just sit here vibrating with my own joy—I have to write about it, I have to share it." David Mason, Poet

I've been practicing Gratitude for over a decade now and this book is my thank you to the universe for putting me in touch with the profound power of Gratitude.

When I was 27, I met a wonderful guy and we fell in love. Life was beautiful. When we broke up, it started a very dark phase of my life.

Gratitude found me and my life turned around. It was all that I needed. I became a Gratitude junkie and today, more than 10 years later, life is great and every day is becoming even better! I have an amazing life, family, job and all areas of my life are bright!

I have a purpose, which is to help millions of people be happier. This is why I wrote *The Gratitude Revolution.*

I would like to ask you to join me in my pursuit of happiness. Let's bring humanity together, let's make everyone we know happier.

Come with me and join the world's next great revolution, *The Gratitude Revolution!*

PART I:
INTRODUCTION TO GRATITUDE

CHAPTER 1:
WHAT IS GRATITUDE?

A brief definition of Gratitude

"Gratitude is not only the greatest of virtues, but the parent of all the others." Marcus Tullius Cicero, Roman philosopher (106 BC - 43 BC)

The first thing that may come to your mind when you hear Gratitude is what your parents taught you about it, that is to be polite by saying "thank you." But that is not real Gratitude, that is politeness!

Gratitude is an immense power that can transform anyone's life into happiness in a second! It is a feeling that spontaneously emerges from within and surrounds you. It is an emotional response and a conscious choice we make.

These are other definitions of Gratitude that can help you understand the power of it:

Rev. Nancy Norman says "Gratitude is a powerful magnetic force that naturally draws joyous people and events to you" and Esther Hicks, the author of several of the most popular books on the Law of Attraction mentions that "appreciation is the purest vibration that exists on the planet today."

According to Jack Kornfield, author of the book *The Wise Hearts*, "Gratitude is a gracious acknowledgment of all that sustains us, a bow to our blessings, great and small. Gratitude is the confidence in life itself. In it, we feel how the same force that pushes grass through cracks in the sidewalk invigorates our own life."

And as Timothy Miller, Professor of Religious Studies at the University of Kansas said, "Gratitude is the intention to count your blessings every day, every minute, while avoiding whenever possible the belief that you need or deserve different circumstances."

Robert Holden, considered "Britain's foremost expert on happiness," said, "The miracle of Gratitude is that it shifts your perception to such an extent that it changes the world that you see."

And I totally agree with all of these people! Ten years ago I started practicing Gratitude and I can assure you at that time I didn't feel like doing it, but I needed to find a purpose and a path out of darkness. Nowadays, every day is a wonderful new day! I wake up full of energy, smile to everyone and behave like a happy innocent child most of the time, which is actually a lot of fun! I go on adventures, I jump in puddles, I laugh loudly and without worries and it's all thanks to Gratitude. Practicing Gratitude has made me see the world in such a different way and in the next chapters I will show you how you can do the same.

Gratitude and Religion

"A great seer once said, 'The angels hover over the Earth looking for the rays of thanksgiving and Gratitude that radiate from a selfless heart.' Louise L. Hay

Over time, Gratitude has been practiced by all the most-recognized religions. Christians, Jews, Muslims and Buddhists all include Gratitude prayers. They all ask to be grateful for every good and bad thing that comes into their life. But in modern days, as many of us are disconnected from religion, Gratitude was forgotten, which led lots of people with perfectly great lives to feel unsatisfied and unhappy. Gratitude is the only thing that separates them from happiness.

Surah Ibrahim in the Holy Qur'an says, *"If ye are grateful, I will add more unto you,"* and one of my favorite quotes about Gratitude comes from Buddha who says, *"Let us rise up and be thankful, for if we didn't learn a lot today, at least we learned a little, and if we didn't learn a little, at least we didn't get sick, and if we got sick, at least we didn't die; so, let us all be thankful..."*

Exercise: What went well today?

"We think too much about what goes wrong and not enough about what goes right in our lives. Of course, sometimes it makes sense to analyze bad events so that we can learn from them and avoid them in the future. However, people tend to spend more time thinking about what is bad in life than is helpful. Worse, this focus on negative events sets us up for anxiety and depression. One way to keep this from happening is to get better at thinking about and savoring what went well." Dr. Martin Seligman, founding father of Positive Psychology

This beautiful story comes from the website Gratefulness.org and it is called Harvesting Gratefulness:

Once there was a very old woman who lived a happy and satisfied life. Many people envied her because of her artistry with life.

The old woman never left her house without a handful of dried white beans. She did not intend to eat the beans, but rather would keep them in the right pocket of her jacket. Every time she experienced something beautiful – a sunrise, a child's laughter, a brief encounter, a good meal, some shade in midday heat – she soaked it up, let it delight her heart, and moved a bean from her right pocket to her left one. When an experience was especially nice and even surprising, she would move two or three beans.

In the evening, the old woman sat at home, counting the beans she had moved. As she celebrated the number of left-pocket beans, she brought before her eyes how much beauty had crossed her path on that day. And on evenings when she could count only one bean, that was still a good day – it had been worth living.

From now on, every night while lying in bed waiting to fall sleep, ask yourself this question: What went well today?

Doing this easy exercise before going to sleep will:

- Make you think about all the good things that happened during the day
- Keep your brain centered on the good while you fall asleep, leaving no space for other not-so-positive thoughts
- Help you fall asleep faster
- Increase the quality of your sleep

I've been doing this exercise since I read it in *The Magic* by Rhonda Byrne, and every time I fall asleep so fast! And whenever I don't do it, suddenly I wonder why I am still awake and then I remember I didn't ask myself what went well today!

Chapter Summary

- Gratitude is a feeling, not a sentence you say to be polite.
- If used right, Gratitude, makes you happier instantly.
- Gratitude has been practiced since the beginning of all major religions.
- Gratitude is counting your blessings every day while appreciating your current circumstances.
- Gratitude draws great people and events to you.

CHAPTER 2:
BENEFITS OF GRATITUDE

"In my 15 years of coaching clients to lead successful, happy lives, I discovered a secret. If I taught them to practice Gratitude, everything in their life transformed... It was as if they had found a magic wand." Sharon Huffman, Coach and Founder of the Center for Empowered Leadership

S o, why would you make the effort to practice Gratitude? What's in it for you?

Positive Psychology is the field of psychology that studies how people can make themselves happier and suggests ways to increase an optimistic outlook. It is a pretty recent field of study, started by Dr. Martin Seligman in the late 90s.

These are some of the results of the research from positive psychology:

- Activities bring more happiness than possessions.
- Being wealthy doesn't make you happier, as long as your income is above the poverty level.
- Grateful people are more likely to be healthy.
- Seeing other people do good things makes us want to do good things too.

Positive psychology research contends that Gratitude is an extremely important positive emotion. So far there's been more than 40 studies on Gratitude that confirm how it benefits us.

In the infographic below you can see a great summary of the benefits of Gratitude:

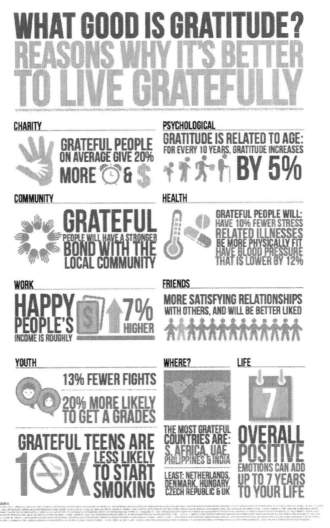

Source: Greater Good Science Center, University of California, Berkeley
http://greatergood.berkeley.edu/article/item/how_gratitude_can_help_you_through_har
d_times

The 8 Main Benefits of Gratitude

1. Gratitude makes you happier

"If you fill your heart with love and Gratitude, you will find yourself surrounded by so much you can love and that you can be grateful for, and you can even get closer to enjoying the life of health and happiness that you seek" Masaru Emoto, Author of The Hidden Messages in Water (1943-2014)

A study performed by Dr. Martin Seligman, one of the greatest proponents of positive psychology, showed that practicing Gratitude for one week resulted in 92% of people feeling happier, and 94% of those who were depressed feeling less depressed.

Gratitude is one of the most effective ways of increasing your life's satisfaction. When we recognize the amazing quality of life that we have, we appreciate it better and we take much better care of ourselves.

A five-minute-a-day Gratitude journal can increase your long-term well-being by more than 10 percent. That's the same impact as doubling your income!

The scientific explanation is when we think positive thoughts like kindness, thankfulness, and optimism, we activate the frontal cortex of our brain, which sends tons of feel-good hormones to our body.

The other explanation is when you are experiencing this level of Gratitude and happiness you start noticing more things to be grateful for and you attract even more! It is that simple. Everybody wins!

2. Gratitude makes you healthier

"Whenever we express Gratitude, we align ourselves with the power that heals us." Daniel T. Peralta, Metaphysical teacher

A study from 2003, "Counting Blessings Versus Burdens" showed that keeping a Gratitude journal caused participants to report:

- 16% fewer physical symptoms
- 19% more time spent exercising
- 10% less physical pain

Also, according to a study published in 2005, "Positive Psychology Progress," a Gratitude journal lowered depressive symptoms by at least 30% for as long as the practice was continued.

So, what are you waiting for to start your Gratitude journal? These are other proven health benefits from practicing Gratitude:

Gratitude makes you sleep better

Gratitude increases your sleep quality, reduces the time required to fall asleep and increases sleep duration. If before you go to sleep you just ask yourself "What went well today?," I guarantee you will fall asleep in less than 10 minutes! Why? Because it makes your mind focus on all the things that went well instead of on what gives you anxiety.

The study from 2003, "Counting Blessings Versus Burdens" showed that keeping a Gratitude journal caused participants to report 8% more sleep and a 25% increase in sleep quality.

Gratitude makes you live longer

Did you know grateful people also live more? When you factor in all the benefits of practicing Gratitude, the cumulative results add 6.9 years to your life. That's right: regularly expressing thanks has been proven to have an even more positive impact on your health than exercising or quitting smoking (but you should try to do those too!).

"Gratitude has the power to heal, energize and change lives" Dr. *Robert Emmons, Professor of Psychology and author of the book "Gratitude Works"*

These are other really important health benefits of Gratitude:

- Grateful people experience fewer aches and pains and report feeling healthier than other people, according to a 2012 study published in Personality and Individual Differences.
- Grateful people are more likely to take care of their health.
- Grateful people exercise more often.
- Grateful people are more likely to attend regular check-ups.
- Gratitude increases happiness and reduces depression.
- Gratitude reduces stress.
- Gratitude plays a major role in overcoming trauma.
- Gratitude also lowers your blood pressure, improves your immune function, and promotes overall well-being.

3. Gratitude boosts your career

"At Whole Foods we practice appreciations at the end of all of our meetings, including even our board meetings—voluntarily expressing Gratitude and thanks to our coworkers for the thoughtful and helpful things they do for us. It would be hard to overestimate how powerful appreciations have been at Whole Foods as a transformational practice for releasing more love throughout the company." John Mackey, American businessman and CEO of Whole Foods Market

- Gratitude makes you a more effective manager.
- Gratitude increases your productivity.
- Gratitude helps you achieve your career goals.
- Gratitude helps you enjoy your time at work more.

4. Gratitude makes you a better person

Gratitude makes you more optimistic

Optimism is correlated with Gratitude because those with an

optimistic disposition are biologically more likely to focus on the good than on the bad. It's been proven that keeping a daily Gratitude journal increases optimism by 15%.

Gratitude makes you less materialistic

What would you say if I told you that doubling your income would only make you slightly happier? Gratitude makes you focus on the things that actually have a much more powerful positive influence on your happiness, like your family, your friends and your health.

Gratitude increases self-esteem

Gratitude helps create a world where people help you all the time with no reason. It has been shown in several studies that Gratitude makes people kinder and more friendly. This increases your self-esteem and makes the world a better place.

A 2014 study published in the Journal of Applied Sport Psychology found that Gratitude increased athlete's self-esteem, an essential component to optimal performance.

Other studies have shown that Gratitude reduces social comparisons. Rather than becoming resentful toward people who have more money or better jobs—a major factor in reduced self-esteem—grateful people are able to appreciate other people's accomplishments.

5. Gratitude helps you find love

"People want to spend time with you if you are a happy person. They don't want to spend time with you if you are an unhappy person." Josh Firger

In a recent study, researchers found out that happy people find (good) marriage partners. Another example of such a "happiness benefit" is that women who express sincere joy in their college yearbook photos are relatively more likely to be married by age 27 and more likely to have satisfying marriages at age 52.

Negativity prevents you from finding love because it is not going to attract someone to you. So, what can you do? Feel happy even when you are still single and do things that you love, because you will find your perfect partner while enjoying life.

Joel Osteen once said that our romantic partners usually fulfill only about 80 percent of our needs. Most people, however, focus on the 20 percent that's missing.

The key is to focus on the 80 percent that is right, wonderful and beautiful about your partner and your relationship and be grateful for it!

6. Gratitude improves your marriage

Do you know what the Losada ratio is? It divides the total number of positive expressions by the total number of negative expressions during a typical interaction in a married couple:

- When the ratio is below 0.9 (there were 11% more negative expressions) marriages end up in divorce or languishment.
- When the ration was above 5.1 (there were 5 positive expressions per 1 negative one) marriages lasted and were found satisfying.

Gratitude helps elevate that ratio by encouraging positive expressions.

Darren Hardy, in his book *The Compound Effect,* tells this lovely story about Gratitude:

One Thanksgiving, I decided to keep a Thanksgiving journal for my wife. Every day for an entire year I logged at least one thing I appreciated about her—the way she interacted with her friends, how she cared for our dogs, the fresh bed she prepared, a succulent meal she whipped up, or the beautiful way she styled her hair that day—whatever. I looked for the things my wife was doing that touched me, or revealed attributes, characteristics, or qualities I appreciated. I wrote them all down secretly for the entire year. By the end of that year, I'd filled an entire journal.

When I gave it to her the following Thanksgiving, she cried, calling it the best gift she'd ever received. (Even better than the BMW I'd given her for her birthday!) The funny thing was that the person most affected by this gift was me. All that journaling forced me to focus on my wife's positive aspects. I was consciously looking for all the things she was doing "right." That heartfelt focus overwhelmed anything I might have otherwise complained about. I fell deeply in love with her all over again (maybe even more than ever, as I was seeing subtleties in her nature and behavior instead of her more obvious qualities). My appreciation, Gratitude, and intention to find the best in her was something I held in my heart and eyes each day. This caused me to show up differently in my marriage, which, of course, made her respond differently to me. Soon, I had even more things to write in my Thanksgiving journal! As a result of choosing to take a mere five minutes every day or so to document all the reasons why I was grateful for her, we experienced one of the best years of our marriage, and it's only gotten better.

7. Gratitude makes you present

"Stop waiting for Friday, for summer, for someone to fall in love with you, for life. Happiness is achieved when you stop waiting for it and make the most of the moment you are in right now."
Unknown

We go through our days living in the future and focusing on what we don't have: a better job, a raise, a baby, a new car, a smaller size ... so hard! Life is so hard! And then you see those who don't have much and are happier than you. Why?

When your today is sorted, that is when you start focusing on the tomorrow to have more, and when we are not living the today, that's when we forget to appreciate what a wonderful world we live in!
The solution? Live today! Be present!

As Lori Harder mentioned once, Gratitude is the quickest way of being present in your life.

"We only have thank you's for your chocolate-flavor moments. We never say 'Thank you' for the things that really, sometimes, have to rub you and push you. and slap you, back into alertness, into your own presence." Mojo, Jamaican Spiritual Teacher

A man was marooned on an island. Each day he prayed for rescue, but none came. With much effort, he built a hut to live in and to store provisions. Then one day the hut burned down. He cried out, "All is gone—God, how could you do this to me!" The next day a ship came to rescue him. He said, "How did you know I was here?" The reply was, "We saw your smoke signal."

This story comes from the book: Gratitude Works!: A 21-Day Program for Creating Emotional Prosperity, from Robert A. Emmons.

Remember the next time when your little hut is burning to the ground, it may be a signal that summons the grace of God!

Living in the past is a waste of time.

"If you are depressed, you are living in the past. If you are anxious, you are living in the future. If you are at peace, you are living in the moment." Anonymous

If you've done something wrong, you cannot change it, so forgive yourself! And if you lost someone, you cannot change that either, so remember that person with love and recover.

Ten years ago I lost someone really important in my life. I was so sad that I would cry every night. After several months like that, I was determined to make a change in my life and every morning I woke up and went for a walk. In the beginning, I looked at one flower, and admired its beauty, leaving my grief behind for some time. Seconds became minutes, hours, days and soon I was able to enjoy life again. I am not telling you to forget, I am asking you to keep on living. There's plenty to be grateful for!

"Be happy for this moment. This moment is your life." Omar Khayyam, Persian philosopher (1048-1131)

Living in the future is not any better!

When you live in the future you focus on what you don't have, which eventually results in anxiety. This ends up making you unhappy, which attracts unhappy things and people. There's no real benefit in living in the future.

Living in the present is the way to go! Be thankful for the opportunity to be living in the present, for appreciating the beauty of the world, people and opportunities!

"By appreciating the gifts of the moment, Gratitude frees us from past regrets and future anxieties. By cultivating gratefulness, we are freed from envy over what we don't have or who we are not. It doesn't make life perfect, but with Gratitude comes the realization that right now, in this moment, we have enough, we are enough." Robert A. Emmons, Professor of Psychology and Author of the book "Thanks!"

The benefits of Gratitude are too enormous to ignore. It illuminates your soul and injects energy and passion into your life. Why not give it a try today? Simply try to actively live a grateful life and you will witness the remarkable transformation it brings.

Exercise: The Gratitude Letter

"You simply will not be the same person two months from now after consciously giving thanks each day for the abundance that exists in your life. And you will have set in motion an ancient spiritual law: the more you have and are grateful for, the more will be given you." Sarah Ban Breathnach, author, philanthropist and public speaker

Sending a Gratitude letter is one of the most powerful exercises you can do and you will remember it forever.

Start thinking about who could be the subject of your letter. It could be someone that you love and admire. It could also be someone you are angry with.

Instructions

- Take a pen and a paper
- Have in front of you a picture of the person you are grateful for
- Start writing down all the things you are grateful for. Don't worry about editing now, just keep on writing.
- Read the letter to yourself and edit if you need to.

Now that you have the letter, you have several options:

- Option 1: Put a stamp on it and send it (lucky her!)
- Option 2: Pick up the phone and read the letter aloud to her (check this video for the results: https://www.youtube.com/watch?v=oHv6vTKD6lg)
- Option 3: Visit her and read the letter aloud in front of her. Don't forget to give her the letter afterwards.

You are going to do great! I am so happy for you! Giving a Gratitude letter is so amazing! You feel great and the person who receives it feels even better! There's only good things that come out of it!

"A few years ago I wrote and mailed a Gratitude letter to a woman who had helped me feel better about myself in childhood. I wrote it approximately 50 years after a particularly helpful incident and wanted to let her know how important her help had been to me not only then, but throughout my growing up years. I did not receive a response from her. But I ran into her niece, a former next-door neighbor, at my oldest brother's funeral, and she made a point to tell me that her Aunt had my letter sitting out in front of her every day and how happy it had made her. Giving back to people who are meaningful is such a blessing. I felt doubly blessed by receiving this feedback, knowing that my letter was important enough to grace her surroundings." Anonymous

Chapter Summary

- Gratitude makes you happier. It also makes you live longer and sleep better.
- Gratitude makes you a more effective manager, increases your productivity, helps you achieve your career goals and makes you enjoy more your time at work.
- Gratitude makes you more optimistic, less materialistic and increases your self-esteem.
- Gratitude helps you find love and improves your marriage.
- Gratitude makes you present. Living in the past is a waste of time and living just thinking about the future makes you focus on what you don't have. Live in the present and be happy for this moment, because this moment is your life!
- Sending a Gratitude letter is one of the most powerful exercises you can do and you and your recipient will remember it forever.

PART II:
A PRACTICAL GUIDE TO GRATITUDE

CHAPTER 3:
HOW TO PRACTICE GRATITUDE

*"We generally do not try to actively infuse our daily experiences
with gratefulness because we sincerely do not know how." Robert
A. Emmons, Professor of Psychology and author of the book
"Gratitude Works"*

L et's talk about what real Gratitude feels like. Get ready for
the power to run through your body and mind! So, what
does Gratitude feel like?

When you feel real Gratitude, a warmth inside you takes over your
body. It starts from your heart and expands to your arms, legs,
neck and head. When you feel real Gratitude, the muscles around
your mouth pull up to form a big wide smile. Your eyes soften and
your forehead raises to look directly to the sky. You feel an intense
current of energy inside. Remember when you were in love?
That's the feeling, those butterflies are pure Gratitude inside!

*"Gratitude is one of the sweet shortcuts to finding peace of mind
and happiness inside. No matter what is going on outside of us,
there's always something we could be grateful for." Barry Neil
Kaufman, Author of the book "Happiness is a Choice"*

I live in NYC and while I am walking to work I practice Gratitude
exercises and feel a lot of Gratitude inside. I start smiling at
everyone and raising my eyes to look at the sky. Then, at some

point, I start feeling a little bit self-conscious for what others may think and I let the Great Feeling go. But I promise you, it is a magnificent feeling. The more you do it, the deeper it gets and the happier and more attractive (in all senses) you become. On top of that, it is free and you can do it anytime and anywhere!

"With all that I have read and all that I have experienced in my own life using the Secret, the power of Gratitude stands above everything else." Rhonda Byrne, Author of the book "The Secret"

Not so many people know that the power to be happy lays inside them. This is also the power that heals us and creates miracles in our lives!

When I hear others talking about me, they use the word "lucky" many times. That's so funny, because Gratitude is what attracts good situations to my life. This is why I wrote this book, because I wanted to shout aloud that Gratitude is the great power for happiness, health, abundance, and luck!

Once you use this power, nothing will be the same and you will live Heaven on Earth!

The first time that you experience Gratitude inside, you may be surprised because the feeling can be very intense. Please don't worry, everything is where it is supposed to be, you are getting in touch with the direct source that makes everything happen. It is great to be able touch the force that has been always inside you.

This is a gorgeous piece from the book "This Ecstasy" from John Squadra about that force:

*"If you listen,
not to the pages or preachers
but to the smallest flower
growing from a crack
in your heart,
you will hear a great song
moving across a wide ocean*

whose water is the music
connecting all the islands
of the universe together,
and touching all
you will feel it
touching you
around you . . .
embracing you
with light.
It is in that light
that everything lives
and will always be alive."

9 Powerful Tips to increase the feeling of Gratitude

After 10 years of practice and countless hours of research, here are nine easy and powerful tips to increase the feeling of Gratitude:

Tip #1: Feel Gratitude inside

"And what will happen? A miracle! You'll find yourself walking around in a state of grace and Gratitude most of the day" Patrice Karst, Author of "The Invisible String"

From now on, every time someone does something for you, say "Thank You." But instead of just saying it, stop for a second, look straight into his eyes, smile and feel it inside. Like a fireball of love you have inside. Feel like you are giving that love to him and smile. You can also imagine sending him a sprinkle of magic Gratitude dust.

The Universe wants you to be happy. Feel the force, feel the life!

Tip #2: Go for the details

"If you want the most ROI from your Gratitude practice the dividends are in the details." Marie Forleo, Life Coach and Author

When feeling grateful for something, always think about why. The more reasons you give the better.

I always use "I am grateful for [...] because [...]." For example:

I'm grateful for [my feet] because [I can walk, I can run, I can jump and I can climb mountains if I want. They make me free to go wherever I want.]

Tip #3: If you have trouble feeling it, imagine you don't have it

If you are having trouble feeling thankful for something or someone, imagine you lost that thing, or the ability of doing that, or that person. For example, if you are having trouble feeling thankful for your partner think about what would happen if you wouldn't have met. Now remind yourself of all the things that you love about him and be thankful for him.

Tip #4: Close your eyes

If you can, while feeling grateful close your eyes. That makes you increase the intensity of the feeling. Remember, the most important part is the feeling. The more intense, the better.

Close your eyes and say for example, "I am grateful for my feet." Then breathe deeply and feel your bones that are holding your body, the skin that protects your feet, the muscles that keep your balance, and connect with that magical force that runs up and down your body and feel grateful for it! Nothing else matters. This moment is yours. Love it!

It's funny. Every time I close my eyes and feel grateful, my neck relaxes making my eyes point directly to the sky while my face muscles pull up making me form a big smile.

Tip #5: Write it down

There's special power in writing down what you are grateful for. You mirror your thoughts on a paper (or an app!), you see them written, and they become real. You give them a mortal existence. Congrats!

When you are writing you are creating. From thoughts to reality, Gratitude becomes more real when you reflect it on paper.

I personally love writing down what I am grateful for. I love to take the pen and write the best I can to create something beautiful, something I am really proud of.

Pro tip: Make sure you have a beautiful notebook and a pen you love. Remember your beautiful thoughts deserve the best.
Now that I am expecting a baby and I cannot wake up so early, I use my commute to write down what I am grateful for in an app. It also works beautifully! At the end of my ride, I leave the train with the greatest smile!

Tip #6: Write down "thank you" 3x at the end

Every time you finish writing down what you are grateful for on paper or your computer or mobile, take the time to write down "thank you" three times. This way you have extra time to go deeper into the feeling.

Tip #7: Read it again

After you have written down what you are grateful for, read it again, if you can aloud. It's challenging not to smile when you do it! Not that you have to be serious, but sometimes it's hard to finish this part because you feel such a wonderful force inside!

Tip #8: Change your routine often

Sometimes you just need to shake it up!

It is important to change your Gratitude routine often so you don't feel like you are doing the same thing every single day. For example, exchange one day of writing what you are grateful for in your diary, for a Gratitude walk in the park.

You are the most important being in the world and you need to make sure you don't burn out. Give yourself lots of cuddles and love and forgive yourself always. You are in the right place and the right time. And you are 100% perfect now.

Tip #9: Gratitude and the Law of Attraction

"Thinking of things you're grateful for is the easiest meditation. Do this for five minutes. Then ask for anything you want." James Altucher, author of the book "Choose Yourself"

Just after you have finished writing down all the things you are grateful for is the perfect time to ask the Universe for whatever you want or need. Why? Because you are in the right frequency that makes things happen! Take this time to ask the Universe for help. It's like you have a direct line with the spirit that makes miracles happen. Use it and enjoy your magical life!

The amazing Brother David Steindl-Rast

"Gratefulness is the key to a happy life that we hold in our hands, because if we are not grateful, then no matter how much we have we will not be happy -- because we will always want to have something else or something more." Brother David Steindl-Rast, Catholic Benedictine monk and Author

Brother David is a Benedictine monk that focuses on helping people understand the power of Gratitude.

His TED talk on Gratitude has been viewed by more than 6 million people and he has created an awesome Gratitude movement all around the world today. This is the transcript of his famous video, "A Good Day." Please, read it and enjoy it! If you can, I totally recommend you to watch the whole video here:

A Good Day by Brother David Steindl-Rast

You think that this is just another day in your life...
It's not just another day.
It's the one day that is given to you – today...
It's given to you.
It's a gift.
It's the only gift that you have right now...
...and the only appropriate response is gratefulness.

If you do nothing else but to cultivate that response to the
great gift that this unique day is...
If you learn to respond as if it were the first day in your life
and the very last day
then you will have spent this day very well.

Begin by opening your eyes, and be surprised that you have
eyes you can open
That incredible array of colors that is constantly offered to us
for our pure enjoyment.

Look at the sky.
We so rarely look at the sky.
We so rarely note how different it is from moment to moment,
with clouds coming and going.
We just think of the weather, and even with the weather we
don't think of all the many nuances of weather...
We just think of "good weather" and "bad weather."

This day, right now, with its unique weather, maybe a kind
that will never exactly in that form come again...
The formation of clouds in the sky will never be the same as it
is right now...

Open your eyes. Look at that.

Look at the faces of people whom you meet.
Each one has an incredible story behind their face, a story
that you could never fully fathom.
Not only their own story, but the story of their ancestors.
We all go back so far...

And in this present moment on this day, all the people you
meet, all that life from generations and from so many places
all over the world flows together and meets you here like a life
giving water if you only open your heart and drink.

Open your heart to the incredible gifts that civilization gives
to us.
You flip a switch and there is electric light.
You turn a faucet and there is warm water, and cold water,
and drinkable water...
a gift that millions and millions in the world will never
experience.

So these are just a few of an enormous number of gifts to
which you can open your heart.

And so I am wishing you will open your heart to all these
blessings and let them flow through you.
That everyone you will meet on this day will be blessed by
you,
just by your eyes, by your smile, by your touch, just by your
presence.

Let the gratefulness overflow into blessing all around you.
Then it will REALLY be a good day.

Expressing your Gratitude

"Feeling Gratitude and not expressing it is like wrapping a present
and not giving it." William Arthur Ward, Author (1921-1994)

In 2016, I met a woman that had problems with her mom. She was stressed because she was going to spend the following two weeks with her and she knew it was going to be a nightmare. I asked her if she had tried writing a Gratitude letter to her mom, because that had helped me a lot in the past. She said that she had even gone further and she had made a painting for her that expressed her Gratitude. Then I asked her what her mom said when she gave it to her. The answer left me speechless. She hadn't given it to her!

Please, don't make the same mistake. If you feel grateful for someone, say it to them. You can do it aloud, writing it or singing it if you prefer! But it is not of any help to keep Gratitude to yourself.

The Greatest Revolution of our Generation

"The greatest revolution of our generation is the discovery that human beings by changing the inner attitudes of their minds, can change the outer aspects of their lives" William James, Philosopher and Psychologist (1842-1910)

Over the last 20 years there's been a continuous change in our collective mind and now more and more people know they have the power to be happy inside.

When you start feeling that you deserve more, stop it, entitlement is at the root of unhappiness. Instead, remind yourself of all the things you are grateful for. For example, sometimes at work we feel we deserve more, a higher salary, more recognition, more! But you will not get those by feeling the lack of them, you will achieve those things by feeling the abundance of what you have right now! A great job, a beautiful office with colleagues that have become your friends, a great company to work for that pays you really well. When you focus on feeling grateful for what you have, more will come!

"What if you gave someone a gift, and they neglected to thank you for it – would you be likely to give them another? Life is the same way. In order to attract more of the blessings that life has to offer,

you must truly appreciate what you already have." Ralph Marston, Football player (1907-1967)

But to change those attitudes you need to change your thoughts and that is the power of a real alchemist, the power to change negative into positive.

"Practicing gratitude, more than penciling a written list, is to practice alchemy. Looking for the good in life literally changes things. Physically changes things. Financially changes things. Mentally and emotionally changes things. It literally rearranges atoms and reconfigures molecules." Pam Grout, Author of the book "Thank and Grow Rich"

Your attitude towards Gratitude

"When it comes to life the critical thing is whether you take things for granted or take them with Gratitude." G. K. Chesterton, Writer and Philosopher (1874-1936)

Your attitude towards the world defines how happy or unhappy you are. You can choose to be grateful, or you can choose to be ungrateful, which means you can choose to be happy or you can choose to be unhappy. It's 100% your choice!

In her book, The How of Happiness, Sonja Lyubomirsky says that 50% of a given human's happiness level is determined by her genes, 10% is affected by her life circumstances, and the remaining 40% is subject to self-control.

This means you can be 40% happier. Let me say it again. **YOU CAN BE 40% HAPPIER TODAY!** And according to Positive Psychology the #1 tool to increase your happiness is Gratitude.

"Gratitude can transform common days into thanksgivings, turn routine jobs into joy, and change ordinary opportunities into blessings." William Arthur Ward, Author (1921-1994)

That's funny because living in New York I see people everywhere, and many of them believe they deserve a better job, more money, more power. That makes them really unhappy, always hunting for something that they don't have and believing when they get there they'll be happy. As Brene Brown (1965) says, "What separates privilege from entitlement is Gratitude."

At the same time, as Frederick Zappone says, "Gratitude is not easy in a society where advertising is written and designed to make you dissatisfied (ungrateful) for what you have in order that you will buy what you don't have."

If you feel you should have more than what you have, please, stop. Close your eyes, breathe and say thank you for the oxygen, feel your body and feel grateful for the warmth of your clothes. Live in the present. Live each second savoring the present moment.

Complaint Free World Inc., has distributed almost 6 million purple bracelets emblazoned with the group's name. When wearers find themselves complaining, they're asked to switch bracelets to their other wrists. The goal is to go 21 days without having to switch.

The author, Will Bowen is a minister with a very simple message: quit complaining. If you do, you'll be happier and healthier. Hence his Complaint-Free World challenge; the goal is to stop for 21 consecutive days. Why 21? That's how long it takes to break a habit, according to Bowen, who has appeared on Oprah and The Today Show discussing his challenge. And while there's no scientific proof his program works, he includes testimonials from people who've stopped their chronic carping and now lead more positive lives.

When you choose to be grateful, to feel grateful, your life changes immediately. It is the most important decision you will ever make. And as Oprah famously says, "If you want to change your state of being, start being grateful."

The hedonic treadmill

"It's not how much we have, but how much we enjoy, that makes

happiness." Charles Spurgeon, Preacher, known as the "Prince of Preachers" (1834-1892)

The hedonic treadmill is the observed tendency of humans to quickly return to a relatively stable level of happiness despite major positive or negative events or life changes. Brickman and Campbell coined the term in 1971 in their essay "Hedonic Relativism and Planning the Good Society."

According to this theory, as a person makes more money, expectations and desires rise in tandem, which results in no permanent gain in happiness.

In simple terms, it means we are never satisfied with what we have. We always want more and we run and run like hamsters on a wheel to find happiness.

We cannot avoid it, but we can be aware of it. Remember, happiness is in the present. It is great to have goals, dreams. It is fantastic. And it has a place.

What if I cannot be grateful?

"There's only one true way to find happiness. That is by controlling your thoughts." Dale Carnegie, Author of "How to Win Friends and Influence People" (1888-1955)

We all have thousands of things to be grateful for but at the beginning, because we are not used to appreciating them, it can be challenging to find them.

Don't worry because the next chapter is all about "What to be grateful for," so bear with me a little bit longer. As Oprah famously said, *"When you think you don't have anything, go back to your breath."*

We all go through moments in life when you are burnt out, angry or sad and we don't really feel like waking up or being grateful. I've had those moments; I thought I would never again be happy.

So start slowly. Look at yourself in the mirror and say, "Hey gorgeous! Good morning" and smile (I promise you, she will smile back!). Love and take great care of yourself. You are gorgeous and perfect today.

Toxic people

"Our minds are Velcro for negative information but Teflon for positive." Dr. Rick Hanson, Psychologist and Author of "Buddha's Brain"

If you're surrounded by negative people and unhappy people, you're going to be negative and unhappy. The same with positive and happy people. To see how others affect you, analyze how you feel after speaking with them. If you don't feel well, you know that relationship may not be the best for you.

You want to be surrounded by people that make you feel happier, more positive, excited about life! As Bahá'u'lláh (1817-1892), the founder of the Bahá'í faith, said "A thankful person is thankful under all circumstances. A complaining soul complains even if he lives in paradise."

Darren Hardy (1971) in his great book, *The Compound Effect,* opened my eyes to the types of associations you have with others. He divides them in:

1-. Dissociations: These are some of the people you need to break away from completely because they have a destructive effect on you. Breaking away won't be easy, but it is necessary if you want to keep on growing and being happier.
2-. Limited Associations: These are the people you can spend a limited amount of time with. That could be up to 3 minutes, 3 hours or 3 days, but no more than that. Identify these relationships and do not allow them to have a negative effect on you.
3-. Expanded Associations: These are the relationships you want to expand and care about. Identify people who have positive qualities in the areas of your life you want to improve and spend more time

with them. As an example, I want to create a successful online business, and I know three people in my network that have done so. The next step is to reach out to them and cultivate that relationship with them. As Jim Rohn said "You are the average of the five people you spend the most time with." Remember you don't have to actually be face-to-face with them, you can read their books to learn more about them!

"I rave about Jim Rohn throughout this book because, aside from my father, Jim remains my foremost mentor and influencer. My relationship with Jim perfectly exemplifies an expanded association. While I got to share a few private meals and spend a little time with him during our interviews and backstage before events, most of my time with Jim was spent listening to him in my car or reading his words in my living room. I have spent more than a thousand hours getting direct instruction from Jim, and 99-percent of that was through books and audio programs." Darren Hardy, "The Compound Effect"

How to change others

Simple answer, you cannot change others. As Lao Tzu said "When the student is ready the teacher will appear."

Don't try to force others to change even if you have the best reasons in the world! People change whenever they want and not before!

That said, there's still something you can do, which is to lead by example.

I remember one morning I was writing what I was grateful for in my journal and my husband walked in. I am always a little bit worried about what he may think because he is not interested so much in these kinds of things. Then he asked me what I was thinking about and I told me I was looking for one thing to be grateful for that I hadn't used before. He started thinking with me and in 2 seconds he said ... PAINT! What? I said. And he continued to tell me for more than 10 minutes all the reasons he was grateful for paint! I was thrilled!!

Your subconscious mind

"Your subconscious mind does not argue with you. It accepts what your conscious mind decrees. If you say, "I can't afford it," your subconscious mind works to make it true." Joseph Murphy, Author of "The Power Of Your Subconscious Mind" (1898-1981)

Psychologists have discovered that our minds are ruled by two different systems—the rational (or conscious) mind and the emotional (or subconscious) mind—that compete for control. The rational mind wants a great beach body; the emotional mind wants that Oreo cookie. These two parts operate on different levels, although they complement each other regarding vital points.

It is often said that the mind can be compared to an iceberg—the small tip above the water is the conscious mind, whereas the huge, unseen 90-percent part of the iceberg that is underwater represents the subconscious.

Think about an elephant and its rider. Your conscious mind is the rider, a little guy on top of a massive elephant, trying to control the elephant while the elephant could do whatever he wants, he's bigger, stronger. What would the rider do to persuade the elephant to do what he wants?

When you train your elephant with constant positive, grateful, and happy thoughts, your elephant becomes positive, grateful and happy. Then the rider lives in harmony with his elephant. Conscious and Subconscious walk towards the same goals and life gets easier.

You cannot be negative and grateful at the same time. It is impossible. You cannot be happy and angry at the same time. It's just impossible, we cannot. So when you use the space in your mind to be grateful, negative feelings don't have any space in your mind and go away.

"Only one thing registers on the subconscious mind: repetitive application practice. What you practice is what you manifest."
Fay Weldon, English novelist

Life is short, you deserve to make the most of it. Your health needs you to be happy, your family needs you to be happy, society needs you to be happy but how can this happiness come to be? It comes with a heart of Gratitude.

What does forgiveness have to do with happiness?

"Holding a grudge doesn't make you strong; it makes you bitter. Forgiving doesn't make you weak; it sets you free." Dave Willis, pastor and author of "The Seven Laws of Love"

My friend Anna was raped when she was 17. She was a virgin then and she felt so embarrassed she didn't tell anyone. She had totally blocked it from her mind and forgotten until 10 years later, in one of our forgiving sessions while remembering it, she started crying. She said she couldn't forgive. She hadn't told anyone. Forgiving meant for her accepting that man and she was not ready for that. After a while, she was able to forgive and her life took off big time!

You may not know what is holding you back. Forgive anyone or any situation that is making you feel bad and as soon as you are done forgiving (patience, sometimes there's lots to forgive), then start feeling grateful and expressing that Gratitude to them. Yes, I said it right! If you've been angry at your boss, I want you to go and tell him that you are grateful for him and for this job that he offered you. Soon everything will start changing, you'll see!

As we come to the end of this chapter we will do a very powerful forgiveness exercise.

Exercise: Forgiveness

"It takes a strong person to say sorry and an even stronger person to forgive." Unknown

1-. Write down on paper ALL the things you've done in the past you are not particularly proud of. Go from your childhood to now. Think about all the areas of your life. Love, health, family, friends, work, money. Now you are thinking "how the heck am I going to feel good after this?" Trust me! You will!

2-. Now, stand up and read the first one aloud. After reading it say: "I deeply and completely love and forgive myself" and give yourself a nice 3-second self-hug (just do it, trust me you will feel great after this).

3-. Go through your list and repeat the process after each item in your list.

4-. Once you are done with all of them, go to a safe place, light the paper on fire and see it burn. See how those things disappear through the purifying power of the fire.

5-. Take it easy after that. You may cry, you may smile, only you know how would you feel after that. Welcome that feeling and love and accept yourself forever.

From now on, every time you feel bad about something you've done, write it down and add at the end "I deeply and completely love and forgive myself." You are perfect, my friend. I truly believe you are.

Pro tip: When you look at someone that you are trying to forgive, imagine yourself giving him a long hug and passing him your love and Gratitude through the 37 trillion cells of your body. Any resistance? Then you need to forgive!

Chapter Summary

- Gratitude is an immense feeling that runs through your body. It is a wonderful current of energy that changes your mood instantly.
- Gratitude is free and you can do it anytime and anywhere.
- Gratitude also heals us and creates miracles in our life.
- There's always something you can be grateful for.
- Tips to increase your feeling of Gratitude: 1) Feel it inside you, 2) Go for the details, 3) If you have trouble feeling it, imagine you don't have it any more, 4) Close your eyes while feeling Gratitude,

5) Write it down, 6) Add "thank you" three times after you say it or write it down, 7) Repeat it aloud, 8) Change your routine often - Don't keep it to yourself, always express your Gratitude.

- The power to be happy lays inside you. By changing your inner attitude you can change your life.

- 40% of your happiness is up to you! That means you can be 40% happier.

- Gratitude is the best tool to increase your happiness.

- If you are surrounded by unhappy people you'll be unhappy. Surround yourself with people who will make you happy.

- You cannot change others, but you can lead by example.

- You cannot feel positive and negative at the same time. Fill your mind with positivity and you'll live Heaven on Earth!

- Forgiveness sets you free. Forgive everything and everyone in your past and make it a habit to forgive every day.

CHAPTER 4:
YOUR GRATITUDE ROUTINE

"We are what we repeatedly do. Excellence, then, is not an act, but a habit." Aristotle, Greek philosopher (384 BC - 322 BC)

Why do I need a Gratitude routine?

You need to have a Gratitude routine because if not, you will forget about being grateful and will lose the awesome effects of Gratitude. Being grateful is really easy, but as Jim Rohn says, "What is easy to do is also easy not to do."

It is really easy to set up a time when you will do your Gratitude exercises, the hard part is to make it a routine, because as studies have shown it takes us three months of constant repetition to fall into a routine. As soon as you pass those three months, you will feel that you need to do the routine always! It will become automatic!

Because here's the thing, as Pam Grout said in her book, *Thanks and Grow Rich*, "When we don't stop daily to inventory all the gazillion things going right in our lives, the crazy voices in our heads try to make us their bitch."

It is like trying to start moving a train. At the beginning, it takes a lot of energy to make it move a few inches, but after a while the difficult part is to stop it!

The best effects of doing Gratitude come when you compound

your efforts. The compound effect indicates that in order to be successful at any venture you need to repeat your actions constantly.

It is extremely easy to take one single action, but it requires consistency to make that action a habit. Actions form habits and habits make you who you are. With Gratitude you want it to become a habit because that's how you'll see the most amazing effects in your life.

How to set up your daily Gratitude routine

"If you don't have 10 minutes for yourself, you don't have a life."
Tony Robbins, Author and Philanthropist

1. Set up a specific time of the day

In order to practice you daily Gratitude you will need to set aside 30 minutes, ideally. Decide when are you going to set that time aside consistently and follow the plan.

I've always preferred the morning because it sets you up for a beautiful day. I usually wake up at 6:30 am and write down in a notebook five things I am grateful for. I try to focus on people instead of material things because I know that increases my happiness the most. Then I also write down daily one thing I am grateful for about my husband. I have a separate notebook where I write his thank you notes and I love looking at him while he reads them as soon as he wakes up each morning. He always has this beautiful smile!

If you cannot do 30 minutes, that's ok! Start with less time, and try to work up to 30 minutes as a goal. Even 5 minutes is better than nothing. The best results I've found are when I can dedicate 30 minutes at once, but the most important thing is to find a routine that works for your life.

Sometimes I wake up later. When that happens I write down what I am grateful for in my mobile during the morning commute, so when I get to work I have a big smile on my face! You can use any note taking app. I use Google Keep.

If you are driving to work, you can use the voice recording app from your mobile and dictate what you are grateful for. After you have finished, don't forget to listen to it because that will make you even happier! Remember, it is always about the intensity of the feeling.

When I include a person in my Gratitude note, I always try to send them the message in a text. The answers are so great! Also you feel happy because you made someone really happy!

2. Track your progress

In order to establish a routine it is useful to have a goal and track your progress. I keep track of whether I did my morning Gratitude routine or not each day. I aim for five days a week, from Monday to Friday.

By the end of the week, I give myself a mark. If I didn't do well I ask myself why and correct for the following week. This helps me keep track and also stay on track.

Darren Hardy has a great book that teaches you how to set up a successful routine and reach any goal. It is called *Living Your Best Year Ever*. It is a fantastic book and it includes a weekly plan to track your progress. It is what I use and recommend. This is the link:
https://store.success.com/shop-all/living-your-best-year-ever-digital-download-edition-by-darren-hardy.html.

3. Allow yourself to be human

It happens. Sometimes you miss a day and it is ok. You will definitely feel that you are missing your Gratitude routine but don't feel guilty or bad about it. Remember you are perfect. Make the conscious effort to go back to your routine as soon as you can and today feel extra grateful for anything that comes your way.

How soon will I see the results?

Gratitude is really effective and fast! From the day you start being grateful everything will be better and you will feel happier.

Gratitude gives you an instant happiness shot. It is all you need to have a blessed life and you can access it at any time!

Exercise: The Gratitude Journal

"The hardest arithmetic to master is that which enables us to count our blessings." Eric Hoffer, Author of the book "Reflections On The Human Condition"

Sabrina Alexis in her article "Giving Thanks: How Gratitude Can Save Your Relationship" relates the next story:

A teacher of mine gave me this suggestion many years ago and I thought it was the most ridiculous thing I had ever heard. I considered myself a very grateful person and did not see how this would benefit me at all. But then I gave it a try and wow...it was not as easy as I expected. My teacher told me to write down three things I was grateful for every day. Easy enough. The catch was that they always had to be different, as in no reruns.

As the days passed and the exercise got a little more difficult, I noticed myself changing. I started to live every day actively looking for things to be grateful for. Usually this was because I wanted to come up with three things and just be done with it, like getting in an early morning workout. I thought it would only continue to get harder but a funny thing happened after a few weeks...it actually got easier. And soon, I was finding way more than just three new things to be grateful for each day. I kept going with this for months and can affirm that it is absolutely life-changing. I felt so calm and so at ease and just happier all around.

How to start writing in you Gratitude journal

How to do this exercise:

1. Decide what time of the day works best for you. I personally prefer the morning because I can see the effects of Gratitude during the day.
2. Buy a really beautiful notebook and a pen that makes you feel happy.
3. Set 30 minutes aside daily to practice Gratitude.
4. Write down five things you are grateful. Make sure they are five different things every day!
5. Add the reason why you are grateful for each of those things.
6. Complete each sentence by adding "thank you, thank you, thank you" at the end.

Try to go as deep in your thought as you can. As Marie Forleo says, "if we want the most bang for our Gratitude buck, we have got to get specific."

Chapter Summary

- Being grateful is easy, but as Jim Rohn said, "What is easy to do, is easy not to do." This is why you need a Gratitude routine.
- Studies have shown it takes us three months of constant repetition to fall into a routine.
- The best effects of doing Gratitude come when you compound your efforts. The compound effect indicates that in order to be successful in any venture you need to repeat your actions constantly.
- To set up your routine, you need to set up a specific time of the day and track your progress.
- Writing a Gratitude Journal has been proven to be one of the best and most effective ways to increase your happiness.

CHAPTER 5:
LET'S EVALUATE YOUR LIFE

In this chapter you will evaluate the state of your life today. This is a really important exercise and it is essential that you complete it to be aware of what may be dragging your energy down.

The exercise is called The Wheel of Life and it was created by Paul J. Meyer, founder of Success Motivation® Institute. It is a powerful visual representation comparing your life today, with how you'd ideally like it to be.

The goal is to find the areas of your life you want to improve and focus on them because an unbalanced life causes stress and can lead to an unhappy life. Happiness is the sum of several areas.

For Gratitude to be part and parcel of your life you need happiness and balance in your life and The Wheel of Life is a simple, but powerful tool to help you attain that. It helps you evaluate your life and discover areas of your life that are off balance so that you can work on it and achieve balance in every aspect of your life.

Because you progress and your priorities change, you need to do this exercise at least once a year. This is why I've created a pdf file that you can do anytime. Here is the link: www.lauramoreno.com/the-wheel-of-life. I hope you enjoy it!

Instructions

This exercise will take you approximately 15 minutes. For each question give a score from 0 to 10, with 10 being the highest score you can get.

Take your time and if you are not sure, choose the first number that came to your mind.

Steps

1) Give a rating from 1 to 10 to the questions below.
2) Divide the total score per section by 10, the total number of questions per section.
3) Place the scores in the chart (round them up or down (for example, if you scored 7.8, write 8 in the chart and if you got 7.1, write 7 in the chart).
4) Connect all the dots.
5) Observe your wheel and analyze the results.

Questions

Give a rating from 0 to 10 to the questions below, being 10 the highest score and 0 the lowest.

Then, divide the total score per section by 10. Do this after you've replied to all the sections.

Section 1 of 8. PHYSICAL

1. I am up-to-date with all my health checks, including my dentist.
2. I exercise at least 3 times a week.
3. I am at my ideal weight.
4. I drink at least 6 glasses of water a day.
5. I am happy and proud of my personal image.
6. I eat 5 pieces of fruit or vegetables a day.
7. I sleep without interruption for 8 hours a day.
8. I never eat candy or fast food.
9. I watch TV less than 5 hours a week.

10. I unconditionally love myself.

What is your total score divided by 10?

Section 2 of 8. FINANCIAL

1. I have 6 months of expenses in cash in case of an emergency.
2. I am out of debt.
3. I have health insurance, disability insurance and life insurance that will cover all my and my family's needs in case something would happen to me.
4. I max out my 401k / IRA contributions every year.
5. I have investments that are increasing my wealth.
6. I use the services of a financial advisor when filing my taxes.
7. I regularly invest in my own training and development.
8. I feel I am compensated fairly.
9. I spend less money than I make.
10. I unsubscribe for paid services that I don't use.

What is your total score divided by 10?

Section 3 of 8. BUSINESS AND CAREER

1. I love my job to the point I could do it without being paid.
2. I continue to improve my skills so I can perform better and become more valuable.
3. I believe my job contributes to make the world a better place.
4. I have clear written career goals and I pursue them daily.
5. I have great relationships with my colleagues.
6. I never gossip about my colleagues.
7. I feel my work is recognized by my superiors and peers.
8. I have a great work/life balance.
9. I look forward to coming to work every day.
10. I pursue my own entrepreneurial ideas.

What is your total score divided by 10?

Section 4 of 8. LIFESTYLE

1. I take holidays at least 4 times a year.
2. I attend cultural events at least once a month.
3. I am constantly trying new and diverse experiences.
4. I live life to the fullest every day.
5. I help at least one person a day.
6. I am completely present in every moment of every day.
7. I pay complete attention when someone is talking to me.
8. I feel I can achieve anything I want.
9. I have dreams and I take time to think about them every day.
10. I am free to do whatever I want any time of the day.

What is your total score divided by 10?

Section 5 of 8. MENTAL

1. I write down at least 3 things that I am grateful for every day.
2. I read something instructional for 20 minutes each day.
3. I've planned my goals and I work towards them every day.
4. All my relationships are a positive influence in my life.
5. I know my life is a present and I enjoy my days to the fullest.
6. I learn about myself every day.
7. I understand I am totally responsible for my situation today.
8. I have a mentor who I trust.
9. I limit my consumption of news.
10. I know how to control my mood.

What is your total score divided by 10?

Section 6 of 8. SPIRITUAL

1. I consider myself a spiritual person.
2. I believe there's something more powerful than myself.
3. I practice my spiritual beliefs daily.
 4. I live completely in accordance with my spiritual beliefs.
5. I use my spirituality to help resolve problems.
6. I teach my spiritual beliefs.
7. I meditate and reflect on my life every day.

8. I accept and respect other people's spiritual beliefs.
9. My spiritual beliefs give me peace.
10. Others who know me consider me a spiritual person.

What is your total score divided by 10?

Section 7 of 8. FAMILY

1. I talk to my family at least once a week.
2. I get together with family at least once a week.
3. There's no one in my family I haven't completely forgiven.
4. I get along well with every member of my family.
5. I take complete responsibility for all conflicts with my family.
6. I always try to be a better son/daughter, sibling, parent and spouse
7. I spend as much time as I want with my family.
8. I am very grateful to have been born in my family.
9. I never gossip about members of my family.
10. I am always available when my family needs my support.

What is your total score divided by 10?

Section 8 out of 8. FRIENDS

1. I talk to my friends at least once a week.
2. I get together with friends at least once a week.
3. There's not one of my friends I haven't completely forgiven.
4. I am 100% happy with the time I spend with my friends.
5. I take complete responsibility for all conflicts with my friends.
6. I always keep on trying to be a better friend.
7. I am still in touch with my childhood best friends.
8. I spend as much time as I want with my friends.
9. All my friends are a good influence in my life.
10. I easily trust all my friends.

What is your total score divided by 10?

Results

Now please go ahead and add your results into your Wheel of Life.
Then connect all the dots to see how balanced your life is.

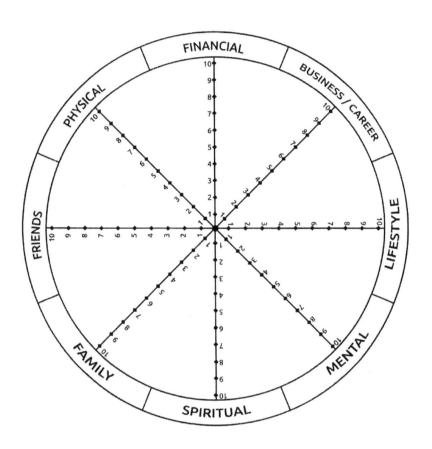

Congrats on completing your first Wheel of Life! How does it
look? Is it balanced? Do you have flat spots?

One thing for sure! Now you know yourself a bit better and
understand which areas are bringing stress into your life.

Are you being grateful for those areas? If PHYSICAL is an area in
which you scored low, are you being grateful for your body right

now? I bet you are not, and that may be the reason why that area scores pretty low.

The same happens for all the areas of your life. I remember few years ago I scored really low in FINANCIAL. I had a terrible relationship with money and I blamed my lack of it on everyone else but me! From that moment onwards I tried to improve that relationship and today, that area is doing really well!

In this book you will find several exercises that will empower you to improve your world. Try to focus on being grateful for the areas where you scored low, and that will make you feel better very soon.

Chapter Summary

- It is essential to know which areas of your life are underperforming in order to take action and create a balanced life.
- Happiness is achieved when you have a balanced life. An unbalanced life causes stress and unhappiness.
- Because your progress and priorities change over time, it's important to analyze your life at least once a year. You can download this exercise here:
http://www.lauramoreno.com/the-wheel-of-life
- After doing the Wheel of Life exercise, look at the underperforming areas of your life and reflect on how grateful you are for those areas right now.
- When you are grateful for all areas of your life, your results and satisfaction in those areas increase exponentially.

PART III:
AN INSPIRATIONAL GUIDE TO GRATITUDE

CHAPTER 6:
WHAT TO BE GRATEFUL FOR

"Don't feel totally, personally, irrevocably, eternally responsible for everything, that's my job." God

It is really easy to be grateful for things. Just stop and look around. It all comes down to changing your attitude inside. The world can be Heaven, just focus on the positives and let go and forgive the rest!

I understand that at times it may not be as easy to find things to be grateful for. At times, it is easy for us to ignore what is going well in our lives and focus on the little things that seem to be off key at the moment. But the truth of the matter is that as long as you are alive, there is hope and if you only cheer up and believe, things will surely fall back into place for you.

To make it easy to classify all the things you can be grateful for, I've come up with a few broad categories, which are: People, Health and Body, Work, The World, and Learning and Growth. There are countless things to be grateful for, so just think of this as a helpful start.

1) People

We are nothing without others, we are a community, we crave talking to others, we love being with others, we are all so similar, soul-brothers and sisters. From your friends and family to strangers, we all come from the same place and we are all here to learn, to have fun and to improve ourselves.

So, why are you thankful for <u>people</u> today?

- Be thankful for your parents whom the universe trusted to take care of you, for all your siblings, aunts and uncles and cousins, all your extended family, all the people that really care about you and who were given as a gift to you.

"Fortunately, our family's practice of Gratitude is firmly in place, which helps us stay connected to one another and to the blessings in our lives. At our house, you have to eat a vegetable and you have to say one thing you're thankful for." Anonymous

- Be thankful for every single friend you have because they enlighten your life!
- Be thankful for every single romantic relationship you've ever had, because you have grown, learned, loved, cried and survived!
- Be thankful for having a loving partner because he or she cares for you.
- Be thankful for all the dating apps because they let you meet awesome people that could share your life!
- Be thankful for sex because it brings you to the stars.
- Be thankful for all types of professionals because they get up early to clean the streets, they prepare your food, they build beautiful houses.
- Be thankful for the kindness of people you've met because they make you happy and inspire you to do the same.
- Be thankful for people you don't like because they make you grow and they remind you how different we all are.

2) Health and Body

"The greatest wealth is health." Virgil, Roman poet (70 BC - 19 BC)

Being healthy is such a blessing that we sometimes forget. It's only when we feel sick that we appreciate how amazing it is to be healthy. Do you remember the last time you were sick? How did you feel? I am sure you were missing those times when you were 100% alright!

Many people after a life-threatening experience have completely changed their lives. Sometimes they leave their stressful jobs to work in something more fulfilling that leaves them more time to spend with their families.

So, why are you thankful for your <u>health</u> today?

- Be thankful because your body is perfect and that can only be explained as a miracle.
- Be thankful for each and every single one of the 37 trillion of cells you have in your body because all of them are healthy. Thank them for doing an amazing job keeping you healthy.
- Be thankful for your bones that support you, for your muscles that make you strong and your heartbeat that creates the music your cells dance along to.
- Be thankful you for all your organs because they exist so you can enjoy this wonderful paradise.
- Be thankful for your brain because thanks to it you can read these words, because it gets wiser every day, because it stores your memories, manufactures your dreams and because you can make them come true.

"The future belongs to those who believe in the beauty of their dreams." Eleanor Roosevelt, American politician and First Lady of the United States

- Be thankful for having recovered from most or all of your illnesses because your body is a magical temple of miracles.
- Be thankful for the fact that your body heals itself every single day!
- Be thankful for all the progress science is making because there are millions of professionals working for you: researchers, doctors, nurses, all of them working for you!
- Be thankful because if you are ill your body might be trying to

tell you something.

"Your biggest symptom just might be your greatest dream trying to break through." Dr. Bernie S. Siegel, Pediatric Surgeon and Author of the book "Love, Medicine and Miracles"

- Be thankful for access to great healthcare, modern medicine, clean facilities, awesome medications that make you feel better because there's a whole industry working for your well-being.
- Be thankful for fun workout classes because they make you feel great while having a great time.
- Be thankful for your face muscles because they let you express your feelings in a gorgeous way.
- Be thankful for your sight because you can observe all colors, shapes, the landscapes and be thankful for another WONDER-FULL day on Mother Earth.

"One July afternoon at our ranch in the Canadian Rockies, I rode toward Helen Keller's cabin. Along the wagon trail I ran through a lovely wood where we had stretched a wire, to guide Helen when she walked there alone, and as I turned down the trail I saw her coming. I sat motionless while this woman, who was doomed to live forever in a black and silent prison, made her way briskly down the path, her face radiant. She stepped out of the woods into a sunlit open space directly in front of me and stopped by a clump of wolf willows. Gathering a handful, she breathed their strange fragrance; her sightless eyes looked up squarely into the sun, and her lips, so magically trained, pronounced the single word "Beautiful!" Then, still smiling, she walked past me. I brushed the tears from my own inadequate eyes. For to me, none of this exquisite highland had seemed beautiful. I had felt only bitter discouragement over the rejection of a piece of writing. I had eyes to see all the wonders of woods, sky and mountains, ears to hear the rushing stream and the song of the wind in the treetops. It took the sightless eyes and sealed ears of this extraordinary woman to show me beauty and bravery." Frazier Hunt from Redbook magazine.

- Be thankful because you can smell a recently baked apple pie, the ocean breeze, grass recently cut, the rain and flowers along your way.

- Be thankful because you can taste strawberries and chocolate, cheese and grapes, ice-creams, new flavors all around the world, be thankful for this amazing blessing that is taste!

- Be thankful because you can feel when someone touches you, kisses you and caresses you, because you are so blessed and so loved.

- Be thankful for being able to hear the singing of the birds, waves, a river going down a mountain, music and the voice of your loved one.

3) Work

"Work is not man's punishment. It is his reward and his strength and his pleasure." George Sand, French novelist (1804-1876)

What a blessing to be able to work, to wake up in the morning and go to work, to have fun with your colleagues, to belong and to improve the world.

In 2009, Doug Conant, then the CEO of the Campbell Soup Company, was in a serious car accident. While he was recovering in the hospital, he received get-well notes from employees across the globe; his wife sat with him and read them aloud. Why was he so appreciated by his employees? Conant did something very unusual for a CEO. He hand-wrote up to 20 notes a day to employees celebrating their successes and contributions. This is what he said about it:

"I was trained to find the busted number in a spreadsheet and identify things that are going wrong, most cultures don't do a good job of celebrating contributions. So I developed the practice of writing notes to our employees. Over 10 years, it amounted to more than 30,000 notes, and we had only 20,000 employees. Wherever I'd go in the world, in employee cubicles you'd find my handwritten notes posted on their bulletin boards."

So, why are you thankful for working for a company today?

- Be thankful for a beautiful office with a comfortable chair and a beautiful desk because it makes you feel great.
- Be thankful for the founder of the company because he created a business that works and that is not an easy feat, my friend!
- Be thankful for your great colleagues because they make you laugh and you learn from them every single day!
- Be thankful for challenges at work because they make you learn, grow, and improve.
- Be thankful for every awesome paycheck you get, because it lets you pay for your food, your house, your entertainment and your warm and beautiful clothes.
- Be thankful for your boss, because she supports you and mentors you.
- Be super thankful for all the free food, snacks and drinks you may get at work, because you don't have to worry about your basic needs at work.
- Be greatly thankful because your job solves a problem of a large number of people and it is a blessing to be able to help people!
- Be grateful for the uniqueness that you and each of your colleagues bring to work because we can all learn from each other and have fun discovering how unique and gorgeous we all are.
- Be thankful because every day you contribute to the overall progress of the company no matter how big or small.

So, why are you thankful for being an entrepreneur today?

- Be thankful for having found a problem worth solving because that is something many other entrepreneurs are looking for and you found it and you are solving it too. Congrats!
- Be thankful for the difficult times when you had to overcome an obstacle, because that made you wiser and stronger.
- Be thankful for having a great impact in the world with your work.
- Be thankful for the freedom being an entrepreneur gives you because you can pursue a new idea any time you want!
- Be thankful for how much you have achieved so far, because you are a hero!

- Be thankful for following the less travelled path, because your days are full of adventures.
- Be thankful for other entrepreneurs that left in writing their wisdom, because you can learn from the best straight away.
- Be thankful for the Internet and how it has lowered the barriers to entry for entrepreneurs because now anyone can start a business and be successful with it.
- Be thankful for the amazing group of people that decided to work with you because they believed in your dream and they keep on supporting you every day.
- Be really thankful for all your clients that decided you were going to be the company that will help them solve their pain points, because they trusted you first over others.
- Be thankful for the excitement of a new idea, because you get to daydream with it and allocate the time and resources needed to make it work if you want to.

- Be thankful for co-working spaces because they give you a fantastic space to expand your ideas and create a community of like-minded people that can help each other grow.
- Be thankful for the mindset and determination that has brought you to where you are because without it you would have followed a path that would not have brought you happiness.
- Be thankful for following your mission and being perfect right now because you are where you are supposed to be and you will get where your imagination takes you.
- Be super thankful for getting to pick the people you get to work with because you get to create your own dream team!

are lucky are optimistic, and optimism is a prerequisite to success in tough circumstances. While that doesn't help in a game of random chance, optimism surely helps in circumstances when you can control the outcome, like when you're building something hard. Thinking you are 'lucky' leads to optimism, which leads to confidence and positive thinking - critical components, along with grit and determination, which actually influence the odds in your favor." Howard Lerman, co-founder and CEO of Yext

4) The World

There's so many things to be grateful for in the World that this section is divided in the following areas: Nature, Technology, Music, Time, Food and drinks, Your home, The World's Diversity, Money, and Animals. Let's begin!

4.1. Nature

"In music, in a flower, in a leaf, in an act of kindness. I see what people call God in all these things" Pablo Casals, Spanish musician (1876-1973)

Everything on Earth is part of this wonderful balance that creates a perfect place for us to live, learn and be happy, and the only appropriate answer is Gratitude.

"Near the end of the war, he was injured in an explosion which seriously impaired his vision. Told that his loss of sight would eventually be total, he decided to return to more familiar surroundings in France to continue his study of music and to prepare himself to leave the world of the sighted. 'The sight of a pin,' he wrote, 'a hair, a leaf, a glass of water - these filled me with tremendous excitement. The plants in the courtyards, the cobblestones, the lamp posts, the faces of strangers. I no longer took them in and bound them up in me, they retained their values, their identities. I went out to them, immersed myself in them and found them more beautiful than I ever dreamed they could be. They taught, they nourished when one gave oneself to them.'"
Robert Ellsberg, Publisher Orbis Books

If you do nothing but observe, admire and be grateful for the world around you, you will be happy and live a wonderfully blessed life.

So, why are you thankful for <u>nature</u> today?

- Be thankful because everything that surrounds us is a miracle!
- Be thankful for the stars because they look at us from above, they make us dream of other worlds and because they guided our ancestors to wonderful adventures.
- Be thankful for the sun because it gives give us the light that warms our bodies and heals us.
- Be thankful for the fire because sitting down in front of it has been one of man's favorite things to do for all times!
- Be thankful for fire too because it transforms wood into ashes, water into steam, and a cold room into a cozy space that brings wonderful people together.
- Be super thankful for rainy days because they clean the streets and they make everything smell fresh.
- Be really thankful for water because it heals us and makes up 70% of our bodies.

"I particularly remember one photograph. It was the most beautiful and delicate crystal that I had so far seen - formed by being exposed to the words 'Love and Gratitude.' It was as if the water had rejoiced and celebrated by creating a flower in bloom. It was so beautiful that I can say that it actually changed my life from that moment on." Masaru Emoto, Author of "The Messages in Water" (Masaru Emoto spent most of his life studying the effect of different messages on water. He exposed two samples of the same water to different feelings and music and then observed their molecular structure. His study is breathtaking!)

You can be thankful for sunrises, sunsets and sunshine, the beauty of nature, a relaxing walk in the woods, a cool swim in the ocean, the sun warming your face, the seasons, the grass that is home for many tiny creatures, snow, rainbows, the Earth, and for so many other beautiful things!

"Regard Heaven as your father, Earth as your mother, and all things as your brothers and sisters." Native American Proverb

4.2. Technology

Technology is amazing! It helps us connect to our loved ones from anywhere in the world, learn whatever we want whenever we want, start businesses, work from anywhere and organize our lives better! On top of that, most of the information and tools online are free!

So, why are you thankful for technology today?

- Be thankful for planes because they let us fly around the world and visit amazing cultures that others could only dream of.
- Be thankful for the amazing access to the Internet because you can learn anything from anywhere for free. How great is that!!!
- Be thankful for Skype because it lets you see and talk to your loved ones for free wherever they are!
- Be thankful for all those people that thought of the things they could create to improve the world. For those who decided to take action and make their dreams come true because thanks to them we can use amazing technology that makes everything easier and faster.
- Be thankful for the group of people that through the years perfected the bicycle, one of the most successful inventions in the world with over 1 billion bicycles around the globe!

Take the time to thank an entrepreneur today, because thanks to his dreams, thanks to his courage, thanks to his persistence, thanks to his imagination your life is easier. Always be thankful for inventors, for entrepreneurs, for people that take the less travelled path. Always be thankful for them!

I was flying the other day and I was complaining to my husband because the plane didn't have movies, and it just hit me! How was it possible? I was flying from New York to Spain in less than 8 hours, 3,500 miles in less than 8 hours! I also realized thanks to planes I have visited twenty-six countries and the only appropriate answer is Gratitude.

4.3. Music

Music touches our senses; it brings us together to listen to something beautiful and powerful. Music touches singers with something more powerful than our own mortality. Music can make you smile, cry, dance. It reaches all the cells in your body.

So, why are you thankful for <u>music</u> today?

- Be thankful for music because it fills your soul in so many different ways and it can make you happy immediately!
- Be thankful for musicians, because they can get in touch with the source of the Universe to create unique beautiful songs that touch our soul.
- Be thankful for the variety of music, from beautiful opera arias to Latin music that makes you shake, from the broken voice of an Andalusian gypsy, to the deep songs of a soul singer.

"Music is said to be the speech of angels." Thomas Carlyle,
Scottish philosopher (1795-1881)

- Be thankful for artists because their art lets you penetrate into their mind and see the world with different lenses.
- Be thankful for all the people in the music industry: composers, singers, musicians, sound engineers, labels, promoters because they bring music to you.
- Be thankful for musicians because they create songs that make your whole body dance to the rhythm of the beat.
- Be thankful for great songs because they create beautiful moments with your friends. Do you remember the last time you were in a car with your friends giving it all to reach that high note?
- Be thankful for musicians because they risk a secure path to let us enjoy their art.

We are an amazing species, we are wonderful, we remember our dreams and then we create them, we let the source of the universe penetrate in our brains to create beautiful things, we are mortal so we push ourselves, we help others. We are one soul divided into different bodies! Remember always to be grateful for that!

4.4. Time

What an amazing opportunity we have living in this wonderful world because it gives us the chance to learn, to try, to fail, to love and to start again!

So, why are you thankful for time today?

- Be thankful for all the time you have had because it is a gift and I know you've had fun!
- Be thankful for the present time, for this moment, right now, because you are blessed and alive.
- Be thankful for your memories with your loved ones, because those will always be there with you whenever you want to cheer up!

"Time has a wonderful way of showing us what really matters."
Margaret Peters, African American history specialist and author

- Be thankful for all your birthdays because those were happy celebrations of your life!

4.5. Food and drinks

"When eating bamboo sprouts, remember the man who planted them." Chinese proverb

I can remember one Thanksgiving when I was visiting my in-law's house in Connecticut. The house was full of sounds and smells. Turkey stuffed with chorizo sausage, beans, gravy, potatoes and lots of pies. Food shared with loved ones. Food that comes to our table from so many different places. Tastes that go from sweet to savory, spicy to bland. Food that is served hot and cold. Contrasts in the flavors, in temperature, in textures and such a beautiful miracle shared with people you love. What a blessing! Food is a miracle, life is a miracle and the only appropriate answer is

Gratitude.

So, why are you thankful for food today?

- Be thankful for all the food you've eaten your whole life because it has provided the energy for you to keep on going until now and that's a lot of food!
- Be thankful for all the things that needed to happen for you to have food. Thank you farmers for planting and collecting gorgeous food, thank you factories for washing and packing it, thank you logistic companies for organizing the transport and thank you truck drivers for bringing the precious food to my supermarket.

4.6. Your home

"I find that the more willing I am to be grateful for the small things in life, the bigger stuff just seems to show up from unexpected sources, and I am constantly looking forward to each day with all the surprises that keep coming my way!" Louise L. Hay, Author of the book "You Can Heal Your Life"

Your home is where you live, where you sleep, where you eat, where you are with yourself and with your family and you should be grateful for every part that holy place. If you ever feel like you don't have enough space, or your things or your house are not nice enough, please remember those that don't have a home and start counting all the things about your home that you are grateful for.

So, why are you thankful for your home today?

- Be thankful for having a roof over your head and walls around you, because they protect you from the wind, the rain and the snow and they keep the cold outside so you can enjoy a perfect temperature.
- Be thankful for your landlord because she decided to rent this beautiful house to you and no other person so you could have a wonderful place to stay.
- Be thankful for a cozy bed because it lets you rest.
- Be thankful for all the furniture you have in your house because

it is all designed to make you more comfortable and happier in your home.

Providing a safe home for those in need is the mission of NewStory, a charity from San Francisco that gives $6,000 houses to those that have been displaced due to natural disasters around the world. Like Charite, a mother of five who had to move to a tarp tent after the 2010 Haitian earthquake. It was too small to fit her whole family so she's been separated from two of her children for more than five years. I encourage you to visit NewStory's website to find out more about them: https://newstorycharity.org/about/

4.7. The World's diversity

"Look at the faces of people whom you meet.
Each one has an incredible story behind their face, a story that
you could never fully fathom.
Not only their own story, but the story of their ancestors.
We all go back so far…

And in this present moment on this day, all the people you meet,
all that life from generations and from so many places all over the
world flows together and meets you here like a life giving water if
you only open your heart and drink."
Brother David Steindl-Rast, author and Catholic Benedictine
monk

Isn't it amazing all the different cultures living together in this world? Think about the Maasai warriors in Africa, the Kazakhs in Mongolia, the Maori in New Zealand and so many other beautiful and different cultures around the world! From Asia, from Africa, from Europe, from Latin America, and even from all the different regions in the United States!

Aren't you grateful that you can experience the beauty of their traditions and even travel to see them in person? Aren't you grateful you even get to ask yourself why they dress themselves like that? And aren't you grateful because just thinking about the whys, your mind expands and opens to other ways of thinking?

So, why are you thankful for <u>the World's diversity</u> today?

- Be thankful for the different cultures we can learn from and can visit all around the world.
- Be thankful for having been born in a city where other cultures live because you can be part of their lives and learn from them.
- Be thankful for the men and women whose mission in life is to bring you the images of these fantastic cultures.

4.8. Money

> *"Focusing on the $3 in your wallet will bring $5 sooner than focusing on the $50 you don't have." Oprah, talk show host and one of the most influential women in the World*

When I was 27 I was in debt and my life was a mess. At that time, my boyfriend lived in another country and all I wanted to do was to leave behind that miserable and poor life and go to see him, but I couldn't afford it.

Those times were hard and I got angry at Money. He was my enemy, the one cutting my wings, the one spoiling my relationship, the one making me so unhappy. I was so angry.

Years later, we made peace. I now understand that Money is my friend. That there's also so much of it everywhere! That you don't have to fight it but be grateful for it! And more keeps coming!

Money is your friend. Take care of him, be grateful for all the money you have and you'll never be poor again!

If you are struggling financially now, think about your relationship with money. Are you grateful for whatever money you have now? Do you treat it with respect? Do you feel there's money everywhere? Are you happy when you find a penny in the street? You should jump if that ever happened to you, because that will tell the universe you are happy when money comes your way, and the universe will send you more!

So, why are you thankful for <u>money</u> today?

- Be thankful for banks because they let us store our money safely.
- Be thankful for all the money you've had in your life because thanks to it you've gone to amazing places, ate wonderful food, acquired great knowledge and had innumerable amazing times with your friends and family.
- Be thankful for all the money you've had in your life because it has allowed you to keep living and enjoying life.
- Be thankful for all the money you have now in the bank and for every single bill and coin you have in your wallet right now because it allows you to have a place you call home, to drink clean water, to have electricity, to be able to call your friends, to have access to an amazing computer in your pocket, for eating out, for taking the public transport instead of walking and for so many other wonderful things!

4.9. Animals

So, why are you thankful for <u>animals</u> today?

- Be thankful for all the animals on the Earth because they remind us of the magnitude of the Universe and its diversity. Like those wonderful exotic birds from Brazil, or the amazing creatures that live in our oceans!
- Be thankful for cows because they give us delicious milk to drink!

- Be thankful for your dog because he loves you so much and asks nothing in return!

5) Learning and Growing

"Flowers unfold slowly and gently, bit by bit in the sunshine, and a soul too must never be punished or driven, but unfolds in its own perfect timing to reveal its true wonder and beauty." The Heron Dance Book of Love and Gratitude

We are in this world to learn and to have fun! The Earth is our training ground and our goal is to improve ourselves, enjoy and leave better than we arrived. That's our ultimate mission.

"We've forgotten that we're here to expand God, to experience joy, to love the holy sh# t out of everything. Instead of laughing and playing and delighting in the Play-Doh, we started taking our lives way too seriously." *Pam Grout, Author of the book "Thank and Grow Rich"*

This is why it is important to remind ourselves that we've been that person we now don't approve of, and that we learned from it. It is really important to forgive. Remember, we are always being moved to perfection.

5.1. Education

"Education is the most powerful weapon which you can use to change the world." Nelson Mandela, South African politician (1918 - 2013)

So, why are you thankful for <u>education</u> today?

- Be thankful for your brain's capacity, because it lets you learn new languages, formulas, concepts and there doesn't seem to be a limit to how much we can learn!
- Be thankful for how affordable education is today because you only have to have access the Internet to learn about whatever topic you are interested in.

"The man who views himself the same at 50 as he did at 20 has wasted 30 years of his life." Muhammad Ali, Prizefighter (1942 - 2016)

- Be thankful for amazing experts that share their knowledge in books and courses because they took the time to teach what they learnt.
- Be thankful for all the opportunities you have had because in the past you couldn't choose your career while now you have thousands of choices.
- Be thankful for having had the luxury of attending a school because that is a privilege not everyone can enjoy.

"In some parts of the world, students are going to school every day. It's their normal life. But in other parts of the world, we are starving for education... it's like a precious gift. It's like a diamond." Malala Yousafzai, Pakistani activist for female education and the youngest-ever Nobel Prize laureate

- Be thankful for all the great teachers you've had in your life because they have shared their knowledge with you with passion.

5.2. Challenges

"Trust that the Universe makes sense. Trust that when it appears you are falling, you are just learning." Julie Keene, American author

Problems are the number one cause of personal growth. Greet them, make them feel welcome because through them you will learn and become stronger and wiser. It is important that we see problems as challenges which are stepping stones to us becoming better, wiser and more accomplished in life.

"When life is sweet, say thank you and celebrate. And when life is bitter, say thank you and grow." Shauna Niequist, author of the book "Present Over Perfect"

So, why are you thankful for <u>challenges</u> today?

- Be thankful for the challenges that have shaped your personality and made you wiser and stronger.
- Be thankful for failure because you learn more failing than succeeding.

> *"By three methods we may learn wisdom. First, by reflection which is the noblest. Second, by imitation, this is easiest. And third, by experience which is the bitterest." Confucius, Chinese philosopher (551 BC - 479 BC)*

- Be thankful for bad days because they teach you it is all about your attitude on life and because you can change how you feel and have a better day!

> *"A bad day is a bad moment that you choose to nurse all day long." Marilyn Sherman, motivational speaker*

6) Others Amazing Things to be Grateful For

6.1. Your Mission on Earth

> *"To bless whatever there is, and for no other reason but simply because it is, that is what we are made for as human beings." Brother David Steindl-Rast, Monk and Author*

What are you here for? You were born with a purpose and only YOU know what it is.

When you are quiet with no worries, a voice talks to you. It tells you that you are in the right place and at the right time now and that you are perfect.

It also tells you what you were born to do, what is your mission in life and that mission is unique to you. You are the only person on Earth that can accomplish it. You just have to trust that everything will be all right.

"The most powerful weapon on Earth is the human soul on fire."
Ferdinand Foch, French General (1851-1929)

I remember that time, that number 300 million... that insecurity, that "how?" It was one sunny afternoon at home. I closed my eyes and there it was: 300. "You are going to help 300 million people to be happier." I also remember the fear, the incredulity, the doubt and the nervousness of knowing that voice was real.

It is great to be working towards your mission because you get this massive energy and motivation to make it come true. The pieces of the puzzle begin to come together at their own pace, sometimes faster than other times, sometimes just imperceptibly. You just have to trust you are being moved towards it. Just focus on your mission and don't stress out about how to get there.

My personal fight is to end unhappiness and negativity. I also want to empower people to become financially free, because I know that's something that many times determines our happiness.

What's your mission?

If you don't know your mission, no worries. Start to know your passions and then choose a fight. There's an abundance of things to improve in Earth.

Here are a couple of hints to know what moves you:

1-. When you go to a bookstore, which section do you go to first? That will indicate what your passion is.
2-. Think about an activity that you do that makes you feel like time flies.

I am not saying you should leave everything you are doing to follow your passion. Don't burn your ships, please. What I am suggesting is that you spend some time doing what you love doing. Just that!

So, why are you thankful for your mission today?

- Feel really grateful because you have a mission, because you can make an impact, because you can help, because you can make others happier. Be grateful for having been born in the lucky side of the World.

6.2. For Everything Happening at the Right Time

"Expect nothing, appreciate EVERYTHING." DeMarcus Betts while incarcerated at the Bellamy Creek Correctional Facility in Ionia.

Everything happens for a reason and what doesn't happen also has a reason. Trust the Universe, let its current take you wherever it wants and believe that everything is going to be well, that you are being moved to perfection!

I believe in the law of attraction. I believe everything you want can become real and I also believe you cannot choose the way that it will happen.

When you practice Gratitude daily for everything and everyone, good or bad, the Universe places fewer obstacles in your way because you are learning, believing, forgiving, being grateful, trusting and letting go. There's still many other things you need to learn, but being grateful you are one step ahead.

Last year I started practicing Gratitude every day and since then great things happen all the time. If I am looking for a new job, I just had to think about it and opportunities start landing from everywhere. The same with money, I set myself a 6-figure salary goal and now I have it. I still had to work for all these things to happen, I networked, applied for jobs and actively negotiated my salary, but positive thinking and Gratitude for what I already had played a really important part in achieving those goals.

One colleague of mine was negotiating her salary at the same time. A few months later we talked again about it and she told me that she was still in the same place, unhappy, unrecognized and earning the same salary as before. When I told her my news, she straight away said that I got a promotion and a salary raise because I was always positive and grateful for what I already had. I wondered if she would start being positive and grateful too for what she already has!

Just love every being and every part of the Earth, forgive and be grateful. Be positive! Be thankful for what you already have today, health, friends, love, money, freedom. You take a sip of water, be grateful, you have a hot shower, be grateful. If you are grateful for everything miracles will start happening immediately to you!

So, why can you be thankful for <u>everything happening at the right time</u>?

- Be grateful because the Universe has always given you what you wanted. Think about it! Always.

6.3. For Every New Day

"Why, who makes much of miracles? As to me I know of nothing else but miracles. To me every hour of the light and dark is a miracle. Every cubic inch of space is a miracle. Every square yard of the surface of the Earth is spread with the same. Every foot of the interior swarms with the same." Walt Whitman, American poet (1819-1892)

Every single new day is an opportunity to appreciate and be thankful for all the beautiful and tasty things around you. Animals, the sun, someone laughing, music, dance! Making someone smile! Learning, sleeping, enjoying life because this is what we are here for!

Gratitude helps you appreciate all great things that happen to you every day and look forward to new gorgeous things every day!

Wake up and say thank you for this day, look at yourself in the mirror and tell yourself how beautiful you are, what a gorgeous body you have! Laugh with your family and friends! Smile to your bosses, help!

Each day is an opportunity to make others happy. How can you do that? You can help others by being happy! And how can you be happy? You can be happy by being grateful.

"That everyone whom you will meet on this day will be blessed by you. Just by your eyes, by your smile, by your touch. Just by your presence. Let gratefulness overflow into blessing all around you. And then, it will really be a good day." Brother David Steindl-Rast

So, why are you thankful for <u>every new day</u>?

- Be thankful because you are going to see the sun again, because you are going to breathe fresh air and because you have another day to enjoy the beautiful world that's been given to you.
- Be thankful because you can enjoy another beautiful day with your loved ones, because you can make them laugh and because you can make them happy.
- Be thankful because you have another day to learn and to follow your great dreams!

6.4. For Gratitude Itself

"Every time we remember to say 'thank you,' we experience nothing less than Heaven on Earth." Sarah Ban Breathnach, Author, philanthropist and public speaker

Don't keep Gratitude for yourself, because Gratitude is a powerful magnet that attracts more to be grateful for. Because it creates joy and forgiveness, because it is the key to happiness!

For more than a year, artist Lori Portka painted her Gratitude through individual pieces of art for 100 people who have made a difference in her life. From her hairstylist to her mechanic, to college roommates to Oprah Winfrey and Ellen, Lori painted bright colorful pieces for those who have brought her joy.

So, why are you thankful about <u>Gratitude</u> today?

- Be thankful for Gratitude because it is an instant cure for unhappiness.
- Be thankful for Gratitude because it is the most effective tool to make others happier.
- Be thankful for Gratitude because you can use it anytime and anywhere.
- Be thankful for Gratitude because it is free!
- Be thankful for Gratitude because it makes others like you.
- Be thankful for Gratitude because you will end up having more!

"Be thankful for what you have; you'll end up having more. If you concentrate on what you don't have, you will never, ever have enough." Oprah, talk show host and one of the most influential women in the world

6.5. For Already Having Everything

"Being so grateful even before you receive, this is the stuff that creates miracles" Christopher Hills, Gratitude: A way of Life

This is a classic story that I love. It's found in many cultures but this version is from Paulo Coelho.

There was once a businessman who was sitting by the beach in a small Brazilian village. As he sat, he saw a Brazilian fisherman rowing a small boat towards the shore having caught quite few big fish. The businessman was impressed and asked the fisherman, "How long does it take you to catch so many fish?" The fisherman replied, "Oh, just a short while." "Then why don't you stay longer at sea and catch even more?" The businessman was astonished. "This is enough to feed my whole family," the fisherman said.

The businessman then asked, "So, what do you do for the rest of the day?" The fisherman replied, "Well, I usually wake up early in the morning, go out to sea and catch a few fish, then go back and play with my kids. In the afternoon, I take a nap with my wife, and evening comes, I join my buddies in the village for a drink — we play guitar, sing and dance throughout the night."

The businessman offered a suggestion to the fisherman. "I am a PhD in business management. I could help you to become a more successful person. From now on, you should spend more time at sea and try to catch as many fish as possible. When you have saved enough money, you could buy a bigger boat and catch even more fish. Soon you will be able to afford to buy more boats, set up your own company, your own production plant for canned food and distribution network. By then, you will have moved out of this village and to Sao Paulo, where you can set up HQ to manage your other branches." The fisherman continues, "And after that?" The businessman laughs heartily, "After that, you can live like a king in your own house, and when the time is right, you can go public and float your shares in the Stock Exchange, and you will be rich." The fisherman asks, "And after that?"

The businessman says, "After that, you can finally retire, you can move to a house by the fishing village, wake up early in the morning, catch a few fish, then return home to play with kids, have a nice afternoon nap with your wife, and when evening comes, you can join your buddies for a drink, play the guitar, sing and dance throughout the night!"

The fisherman was puzzled, "Isn't that what I am doing now?"

He's so right! We are always chasing what we don't have. Just stop and appreciate your life today.

A month ago I told my husband I needed a weekend alone to write this book. That I needed to be in a peaceful place surrounded by nature, by abundance, by beautiful music and by quietness.

I told him that I needed it, that it was essential, that I was going to take that weekend off and rent a cabin somewhere in the woods.

And here I am today. The reality is that I didn't take that weekend off or book that place. And as I was thinking about that, I look around and I just realize that I am sitting in a house surrounded by the woods, listening to the beautiful music of Chopin writing this book while visiting my family. That everything that I asked for weeks ago is in front of me today. A massive grateful feeling has taken my body and I am now crying.

And I realized that we have EVERYTHING we ask for. EVERYTHING! That life is a great friend and that it gives you everything you want. That when was the last time something I wanted didn't happen? That ALL that I ask for is given to me. That everything is so perfect today, that I don't need anything else!

Thank you Universe. I love you and you love me. I love you life, we are friends, no better, we are the same!

Thank you, thank you, thank you for this year studying gratitude, thank you for every single morning I wake up earlier to be grateful because we understand each other, because we love each other because we are one.

Listen my dear friend, the Universe wants to you be happy, and to be happy you need to be grateful. If you are grateful you will love others, if you love others, they will love you back. Know that this is a beautiful cycle that starts with Gratitude and trust, all the rest will come.

The Universe wants to give you everything that you want because you will be happier and as we are all part of the Universe, the Universe will be happier too!

To be happy, be grateful, love your life, love others and smile. Yes, give me that big smile!

Trust and let go.

Forgive and love.

Exercise: Gratitude Walk

Instructions

- Find sometime in your day and go out for a walk, ideally somewhere surrounded by nature.
- While you walk, start feeling grateful for your body. For example say "thank you feet because you take me to wonderful places in the world," and keep on doing the same for each part of your body. From your feet to your head. There's so much to be grateful for!
- Continue being grateful about your surroundings. Look at the beautiful world you live in and one by one say thank you to the things around you. Look at the Sun, and say thank you Sun because ...
- And finish by being grateful for the people around you: your family, your partner, your friends and go one by one saying "thank you [...] because [...]." Sometimes it becomes more challenging when you cannot be thankful for someone. And that's okay. Forgive, let go and tomorrow you can try again.

By the end of this exercise you will feel so great! And remember that to bring blessings and abundance to your life the most important part is what you feel when you are grateful. That is the magic power that attracts love, abundance and happiness.

"To experience deep gratitude, sit down and write a list of things you are grateful for. Keep writing your list until your eyes are overflowing with tears. As the tears come, you will feel the most beautiful feeling around your heart and all through the inside of you. This is the feeling of true gratitude. You have felt this feeling you will know how to re-create it. This intense feeling of gratitude is the feeling you want to reproduce as many times a day as you can." Rhonda Byrne, Daily Teachings of The Secret, Day 57

Chapter Summary

- It is really easy to be grateful for things. Just stop and look around! There's millions of things to be grateful for!
- Make it a habit to appreciate everything you've been given today. That will change your life from the moment you start.
- When being grateful for something always add the "why" after. That will make you go deep into the feeling.

REVIEW REQUEST

The goal of this book is to make millions of people happier with the power of Gratitude and you are one of them!

I really hope after reading this book YOU are happier and have the necessary tools to make a paradise on Earth for yourself. I've written all I know about how it works with only that one goal, to make you happier.

Now, in order to reach more people I need your help ;-) Reviews are the key to the success of a book on Amazon. The more honest reviews this book receives, the more people will read it.

If you enjoyed this book and found it useful, I'd be very, very, very grateful if you'd post an honest review on Amazon. Your support really matters to me so much (it really makes a massive difference) and you'll help others be happier too!

Please, leave a review today!

All you need to do is to go to the review section on this book's Amazon page: http://bit.ly/thegratitudebook. You'll see a big button that says "Write a customer review" - click that and you're good to go!

Thanks again for your support. With Love and Gratitude! <3

Laura Moreno

BIBLIOGRAPHY

365grateful | Stories About the Extraordinary Power of Gratitude. (2017). *365 Grateful*. Retrieved 21 March 2017, from http://365grateful.com/

Alexis, S. (2017). *Giving Thanks: How Gratitude Can Save Your Relationship*. Retrieved 3 February 2017, from http://www.anewmode.com/dating-relationships/giving-thanks-how-gratitude-can-save-your-relationship/

Amin, A. (2017). *The 31 Benefits of Gratitude You Didn't Know About: How Gratitude Can Change Your Life*. *HappierHuman*. Retrieved 11 March 2017, from http://happierhuman.com/benefits-of-gratitude/

Bailey, C., & Bailey, C. (2017). *100 things to be grateful for – A Life of Productivity*. *Alifeofproductivity.com*. Retrieved 23 February 2017, from http://alifeofproductivity.com/100-things-to-be-grateful-for/

Bentley College Commencement Speech. (2017). *Whole Foods Market*. Retrieved 21 March 2017, from http://www.wholefoodsmarket.com/blog/john-mackeys-blog/bentley-college-commencement%C2%A0speech

Cisek, J. (2017). *Conscious vs subconscious processing*

power. Retrieved 3 February 2017, from http://spdrdng.com/posts/conscious-vs-subconscious-processing

Cite a Website - Cite This For Me. (2017). *Meettomarry.com*. Retrieved 11 March 2017, from http://meettomarry.com/how-can-gratitude-help-you-find-true-love/

Double page pumpkin Secret Garden. Página dupla Jardim Secreto. (2017). *Pinterest*. Retrieved 21 March 2017, from https://www.pinterest.com/pin/523543525409382489/

Elie Wiesel Quotes. (2017). *BrainyQuote*. Retrieved 21 March 2017, from https://www.brainyquote.com/quotes/quotes/e/eliewiesel5997 68.html

Forbes Welcome. (2017). *Forbes.com*. Retrieved 29 January 2017, from http://www.forbes.com/sites/augustturak/2011/08/05/a-leadership-lesson-from-meister-eckhart/#3ac4916951f0

Forbes Welcome. (2017). *Forbes.com*. Retrieved 21 March 2017, from http://www.forbes.com/sites/amymorin/2014/11/23/7-scientifically-proven-benefits-of-gratitude-that-will-motivate-you-to-give-thanks-year-round/

Forleo, M. (2016). *Gratitude: The Most Powerful Practice You're Not Doing. YouTube*. Retrieved 17 October 2016, from https://www.youtube.com/watch?v=eFqsUow-HvM

Gratitude. (2017). *Pinterest*. Retrieved 21 March 2017, from https://www.pinterest.com/pin/28851253834667858/

GRATITUDE. (2017). *EAT THE CAKE FIRST*. Retrieved 21 March 2017, from http://www.choosingratitude.com/gratitude.html

Gratitude Letter (Greater Good in Action). (2017). *Ggia.berkeley.edu*. Retrieved 21 March 2017, from http://ggia.berkeley.edu/practice/gratitude_letter

Grout, P. *Thank & Grow Rich* (1st ed.).

Hamid, S. (2017). *The Science of Shukr. Shukr.co.uk*. Retrieved 21 March 2017, from http://www.shukr.co.uk/blog/index.php/2014/11/the-science-of-shukr/

Happiness Quotes - Finding Happiness. (2017). *Finding Happiness*. Retrieved 29 January 2017, from http://findinghappinessmovie.com/find-happiness/happiness-quotes/

Hardy, D. (2011). *Living Your Best Year Ever* (1st ed.). Success Media Books.

Hardy, D. (2016). *Darren Hardy | To Be Great, Be Grateful. Darrenhardy.com*. Retrieved 17 October 2016, from https://darrenhardy.com/2010/11/to-be-great-be-grateful/

Hedonic treadmill. (2017). *En.wikipedia.org*. Retrieved 3 February 2017, from https://en.wikipedia.org/wiki/Hedonic_treadmill

Isabelle's Gift. (2017). *The Huffington Post*. Retrieved 21 March 2017, from http://www.huffingtonpost.com/kathleensmith/meet-the-morphmoms_4_b_5351792.html

Jeffers, S. (1987). *Feel the fear and do it anyway* (1st ed.). San Diego: Harcourt Brace Jovanovich.

KilClark, C. (2017). *7 Benefits of Practicing Gratitude Every Day. Carin Kilby Clark.* Retrieved 21 March 2017, from https://carinkilbyclark.com/benefits-practicing-gratitude/

Lesowitz, N., & Sammons, M. (2009). *Living life as a thank you* (1st ed.). San Francisco, Calif.: Viva Editions.

Lyubomirsky, S. (2008). *The how of happiness.* New York: Penguin Press.

Lyubomirsky, S. (2016). *Discover Happiness | The How of Happiness. Thehowofhappiness.com.* Retrieved 19 October 2016, from http://thehowofhappiness.com/discover-happiness/

Madeline R. Vann, M. (2017). *The Power of Positive Psychology. EverydayHealth.com.* Retrieved 11 March 2017, from http://www.everydayhealth.com/emotional-health/understanding/the-role-of-positive-psychology.aspx

Murphy, J., & Pell, A. (2008). *The power of your subconscious mind* (1st ed.). New York: Prentice Hall Press.

Nonfiction Book Review: A Complaint-Free World: How to Stop Complaining and Start Enjoying the Life You Always Wanted by Will Bowen, Author. Doubleday $18.95 (192p) ISBN 978-0-385-52458-2. (2017). *PublishersWeekly.com.* Retrieved 3 February 2017, from http://www.publishersweekly.com/978-0-385-52458-2

Oprah's Gratitude Journal | Oprah's Lifeclass | Oprah Life Lessons Winfrey Network. (2016). *YouTube.* Retrieved 19 October 2016, from https://www.youtube.com/watch?v=JzFiKRpsz8c&feature=youtu.be

Parabola Magazine • *"When a person doesn't have gratitude, something....* (2017). *Parabola Magazine*. Retrieved 21 March 2017, from http://parabola-magazine.tumblr.com/post/146831363426/when-a-person-doesnt-have-gratitude-something

Priorities. (2017). *THE 11-10-02 FOUNDATION*. Retrieved 21 March 2017, from http://www.shakingupamerica.org/priorities.html

Research. (2017). *Project Thankful Heart*. Retrieved 21 March 2017, from https://projectthankfulheart.com/research/

Seligman, M. *Flourish* (1st ed.).

Shah,. (2017). *WORK LIFE BALANCE*. *Slideshare.net*. Retrieved 29 January 2017, from http://www.slideshare.net/akshah333/work-life-balance-29701244

Starting a Gratitude Practice - Planet Beach spray & spa. (2017). *Planet Beach spray & spa*. Retrieved 21 March 2017, from http://planetbeach.com/wellness-tips/starting-gratitude-practice/

Steindl-Rast, D. (2017). *David Steindl-Rast | Speaker | TED.com*. *Ted.com*. Retrieved 31 January 2017, from https://www.ted.com/speakers/br_david_steindl_rast

Stuff, T. (2017). *25 Entrepreneurs, Including 2 Sharks, Share What They're Thankful ForTrue Viral News | True Viral News*. *Trueviralnews.com*. Retrieved 21 March 2017, from http://trueviralnews.com/25-entrepreneurs-including-2-sharks-share-what-theyre-thankful-for/

Switch - Heath Brothers. (2017). *Heath Brothers*. Retrieved 3 February 2017, from http://heathbrothers.com/books/switch/

Teachers who inspire.... (2017). *Everything Matters: Beyond Meds*. Retrieved 21 March 2017, from https://beyondmeds.com/2012/10/25/teachers-who-inspire/

The Concept of Thankfulness in Islam. (2016). *WhyIslam*. Retrieved 19 October 2016, from https://www.whyislam.org/on-faith/the-concept-of-gratitude-in-islam/

To know even one life has breathed easier because you have lived, this is to have succeeded. - philosiblog. (2017). *philosiblog*. Retrieved 21 March 2017, from http://philosiblog.com/2013/03/13/to-know-even-one-life-has-breathed-easier-because-you-have-lived-this-is-to-have-succeeded/

Tobin, N. (2017). *Benefits of Keeping a Daily Journal to Improve Productivity*. *Nora Tobin*. Retrieved 21 March 2017, from http://www.noratobin.com/benefits-keeping-journal-rapidly-improve-performance/

Understanding the Conscious vs Subconscious Mind in 4 Steps - Operation Meditation. (2017). *Operation Meditation*. Retrieved 3 February 2017, from http://operationmeditation.com/discover/understanding-the-conscious-vs-subconscious-mind-in-4-steps/

What is Gratitude? - Gratefulness.org. (2016). *Gratefulness.org*. Retrieved 19 October 2016, from http://gratefulness.org/resource/what-is-gratitude/

Why (and how) You Should Practice Gratitude Every Day. (2017). *The Frugal Model*. Retrieved 21 March 2017, from http://thefrugalmodel.com/practice-gratitude/

63516599R00064

Made in the USA
Lexington, KY
09 May 2017